POTJIEKOS
FAVOURITES

Struik Lifestyle
(an imprint of Random House Struik (Pty) Ltd)
Company Reg. No. 1966/003153/07
80 McKenzie Street, Cape Town 8001
PO Box 1144, Cape Town, 8000, South Africa

www.randomstruik.co.za

First published in 1988 by Struik Publishers
Second edition published in 2000
Reprinted in 2001, 2002, 2003, 2005, 2006, 2007, 2008

Publisher: Linda de Villiers
Concept designer: Christelle Nothnagel
Editor: Joy Clack
Illustrator: Basil Juries
Photographer: Willie van Heerden

Reproduction: Hirt & Carter Cape (Pty) Ltd
Printing and binding: CTP Book Printers (Pty) Ltd

ISBN 978-1-86872-434-5

Contents

Foreword

Potjiekos has been with us for centuries, in fact since the days of the first settlement at the Cape when food was cooked in a black cast-iron pot hanging from a chain over the kitchen fire. Later the black pot accompanied those intrepid pioneers who moved into our hinterland, but as the Victorian era unfolded, so the delights of the bubbling black pot made way for magnificent oven roasts, and later still the traditional braaivleis in the 1950s and '60s. The pot's re-emergence in the late 1970s coincided with the escalation of meat prices and it was then that *Sarie* became the first magazine to publish articles on the art of potjiekos cooking, which resulted in a wave of books on the subject.

South Africans have become much more food conscious than many people seem to realize and we love good, honest cooking, as well as substantial and satisfying meals. It is around an open fire, preferably in convivial company, with one or more potjies simmering away that these prerequisites are met.

This special collection of recipes is a celebration of my friend, the late Sannie Smit. Many of these are classic or regional recipes, which reflect our great culinary heritage, while others have been newly developed. Above all, this book reveals an affordable way of cooking and one that is uniquely South African.

Peter Veldsman
Former food editor of *Sarie*
Cape Town 1988

Introduction

I grew up with potjiekos on a farm in the northern Cape where life was simpler and honest country cooking was enjoyed to the full. In particular I remember the slaughter-day potjie. Everything, including the liver and the tripe, was simmered in one big black pot to make a tasty and wholesome stew. As children, we would also have our own potjie far away from the house where mother couldn't see us. Often an empty jam tin was used as a stewpot for these concoctions, which we made with anything from a few stolen slices of the Sunday roast to a small, troublesome bird killed with a home-made catapult.

Potjiekos is a friendly food, to be enjoyed by rich or poor, young and not so young, city-dwellers and country folk, needing only one's imagination when it comes to selecting the ingredients. It's the ideal food to serve to a crowd and its popularity in recent years can be attributed to its versatility and relatively low cost. With the revival of potjiekos, we can again sit companionably around a fire as the potjie simmers away.

But where did the original potjiekos come from? No one seems to be able to pinpoint the exact origin with any accuracy and there are many theories. It seems that it might be a legacy from our Dutch ancestors who brought with them heavy iron cooking pots, which hung from hooks over the open hearth. These cast-iron pots retained heat well and could be kept simmering over a few embers. Rounded, pot-bellied pots were used for cooking tender roasts and stews as they allowed steam to circulate instead of escape through the lid, while flat-bottomed iron pans heated more quickly and were used to bake crusty loaves of bread in Dutch ovens.

What sets potjiekos apart from these traditional cooking methods, is the fact that it is cooked outside. When the pot was moved from the kitchen hearth to a fire in the open veld, it became a 'potjie' and part of our cooking heritage. The potjie filled a specific need when the Trekkers started moving north. You couldn't take a kitchen and a stove along on the trek and so the portable, three-legged, cast-iron potjie took the place of these cooking facilities. The potjie's convenient handle meant it could be hung up inside or on the outside of the wagon, without any danger of it falling over and spilling its contents during the trek. Having three legs, a potjie can stand practically anywhere. It didn't matter where the Trekkers stopped. A small fire could quickly be made on the ground wherever they happened to be and there was no need to find stones to support the potjie. The old-fashioned trekpotjie was used in much the same way as a French stock pot, or *marmite* (also a round-bellied pot), which bubbled on the stove all day and to which you continuously added anything that was available. Usually, the only meat available on a trek was an old trek-ox, mutton or game shot along the trail. This meat was always tough and certainly not suitable for grilling over glowing coals. It needed long, slow simmering to make it palatable and so potjiekos came into being. Who knows, maybe the 'thin layers' and 'don't stir' rules originated here.

In the not-too-distant past, it was still the custom in certain areas of our country, such as the north-eastern Cape, to make *trekkos* during the seasonal trek with the cattle from the summer to the winter farm. *Trekkos* is a dish consisting of mutton, onions and potatoes cooked together in a three-legged potjie. The ingredients are layered and highly seasoned with pepper, a method thought to preserve the contents and to discourage flies and other insects. At the end of the day the meal could be served cold or it could be heated over a small fire.

On the West Coast, potjiekos is made with crayfish and other seafood. Although I wonder if a three-legged cast-iron potjie is used at all or if they don't simply use a *konka,* in which the crayfish is boiled in seawater.

The cast-iron three-legged potjie made its way into African tribal culture as the porridge pot and still to this day, everything, from porridge and springhare to fat mopani worms, is cooked in the traditional potjie, using any available fuel, be it dung, renosterbos or vaalbos twigs. It is sad that this custom is gradually dying out due to urbanization.

While there are many South Africans, especially in rural communities, who have upheld the potjie tradition over the years, it is only in fairly recent times that cooking in a cast-iron pot over an open fire has gained wide popularity. Although we owe this revival of potjiekos to a number of experts, I would like to single out Peter Veldsman, former food editor of *Sarie*. Peter encouraged his readers, over a period of several years, to send in their favourite, local recipes. This series on South African regional food led to the rediscovery of a marvellous food culture that might otherwise have been lost forever.

Nowadays, our busy lifestyles often prevent us from getting together with friends and family for leisurely, companionable meals. Potjiekos has changed all that: it affords the opportunity once again to relax and enjoy a few hours in the easy, sociable atmosphere that develops around the bubbling pot. It's an event in which everyone can participate: husbands, wives, children, aunts, uncles, grandmothers, grandfathers and friends, old and young. Someone to peel the vegetables, another to look after the fire, and yet another to keep an eye on the pot, while the music-makers and the 'cupbearers of Bacchus' look after the drinks and make sure the atmosphere stays at its convivial best.

It's a simple style of cooking with no airs and graces, using everyday ingredients to produce wholesome one-pot meals. Most of the recipes in this book are relatively simple, and a fair amount of them, such as the bredies, are based on traditional Cape cooking, while the use of ginger, garlic and spices reflects the Malay and Indian influences.

Potjiekos is really the epitome of South African hospitablity: good food, good wine and good company.

Ingredients

When it comes to potjiekos, the recipes, rules and regulations are only there to guide you, so you don't have to follow them blindly. The imaginative use of ingredients is the thing that really counts, as potjiekos recipes are nearly always created and prepared according to what's available.

Remember too, that the aroma and flavour of the main ingredient should not be overpowered; the other ingredients are added simply to enhance the flavour. If you use too many different vegetables, garnishes and side dishes in relation to the main ingredient, the subtle blend of flavours will be lost and what might have been a delicious meal will turn into something rather less than enjoyable.

Meat

Potjiekos works on the moist-heat cooking principle where moisture is formed during the cooking process. The best meat cuts to use in potjiekos are the economical cuts with a high percentage of white connective tissue (sinews), which become tender and gelatinous when simmered for a long time to develop the flavour. These cuts are, therefore, more suitable than fillet and sirloin, which are, in any case, much too expensive to use for potjiekos.

Furthermore, it's not necessary to buy only choice cuts from the higher grades for potjiekos, although one has to admit that meat of good quality does make a difference to the end result. For maximum flavour it is best to use meat such as brisket, shin, and neck, sawn into pieces.

The meat for potjiekos does not have to be ripened, unlike choice beef cuts used for grilling or roasting. Not all meat takes hours to cook so if you are in a hurry, opt for mince, chicken or fish.

The most suitable cuts of meat are:

Beef: Bolo; neck; chuck; hump; flat rib; brisket; shin; thin flank with short rib; thick flank; silverside; aitchbone; oxtail; topside; mince

Lamb and Mutton: Neck; thick rib; raised shoulder; leg; flank; breast; shank (from the shoulder and leg); knuckles

Pork: Head; thick rib; breast; shin and trotter; flank; short rib

Offal: Liver (ox, sheep's and game); heart (ox and sheep's); kidneys (ox, game and pig); tripe (ox and sheep); trotters (ox, sheep's and calf's); sheep's head; sweetbread

Poultry

Poultry of any kind is suitable for all kinds of potjiekos, from creamy stews to fruity curries. Available conveniently cut into portions, chicken is quick-cooking and can be prepared in a number of different ways. Its flavour is enhanced by the addition of herbs, fruit, bacon, wine, mushrooms, tomatoes and spices. The moist-heat method of cooking is also ideal for turkey, as the flesh tends to be dry. Turkey is now available throughout the year from major supermarkets and makes an economical alternative to chicken.

Venison and game birds

Both are excellent for potjiekos. Because the meat tends to be dry, a piece of spek or fatty breast of mutton should always be added, or even, if available, a fatty sheep's tail. The addition of red wine, or a little cream or butter beaten into the gravy will do wonders for the flavour and texture.

Fish

Snoek, tuna, swordfish, butterfish, kabeljou, kingklip, squid and octopus are firm fish and are, therefore, suitable for potjiekos. Hake and sole are less suitable because they tend to fall apart easily. Oysters, mussels, crayfish and prawns also make very tasty potjiekos. Don't make the mistake of overcooking these delicious seafoods. Remove scales, skin and as many bones as possible before cooking fish.

Vegetables

Vegetables, either as a side dish or as a main course, are delicious when prepared in a potjie. Many of our traditional vegetables, such as sweet potatoes and pumpkin, make excellent potjiekos. These should be cooked in a flat-bottomed potjie, while vegetable stew would be better cooked in a three-legged potjie. The pungent and aromatic onion acts as both a flavouring agent and as a vegetable in its own right and is indispensable in potjiekos cooking.

When cooking a variety of vegetables in one pot, one shouldn't combine too many strongly flavoured vegetables. The same applies to using delicately and strongly flavoured vegetables together. The flavour of the main ingredient must always be dominant. Take care too, that the flavours blend. For instance, cabbage and sweet potatoes don't go together very well. Remember when arranging the vegetables to place those that take the longest to cook in the potjie first.

Pulses

Dried beans, peas and lentils are classified as 'pulses'. There are hundreds of varieties with different flavours and textures, and these are all regarded as a good source of protein. Readily available from supermarkets and health-food stores, they have a long shelf life and make delicious soups and main course dishes. They are an ideal potjiekos ingredient whether used to help stretch the menu or as the main ingredient in a vegetarian dish. Though economical and easy to prepare, pulses tend to be bland in taste unless added to a well-flavoured meaty stew or a seasoned stock. Adding tomatoes or wine too soon will toughen beans, so leave these ingredients out until near the end of the cooking time.

Most beans need soaking to restore the water lost during drying. Beans may be soaked using one of the two methods below:

Quick soaking: Place beans in a large potjie, add cold water to cover and bring to the boil. Cover potjie with lid and cook for 5 minutes, then remove from heat. Allow to stand for 1 hour, then drain and cook according to the recipe.

Overnight soaking: Place beans in a large bowl, cover with cold water and soak for 6–8 hours, but no longer. Drain and cook according to the recipe.

Seasoning

Salt and freshly ground black pepper are the most important seasonings for potjiekos. A sprinkling of herbs added towards the end of the cooking time adds a touch of magic to food, but must be used sparingly. Don't be tempted to use too many together; the flavours should blend and not compete with each other. If you don't have access to fresh herbs, dried herbs can also be used to great effect: simply remember to use smaller quantities because the flavour is more concentrated. Other seasonings include garlic, lemon juice and soy sauce.

Liquid

A common mistake is to add too much liquid to the pot. It is best to add sufficient to keep the pot bubbling and to top it up from time to time. Whichever liquid is used, remember that plain water adds no flavour to a dish, so rather use a flavoursome liquid. Have a small potjie (No. $3/4$ or 1) on hand for heating up the liquid before adding it to the browned meat in the potjie, as meat juices will be extracted and the meat itself will be dry if cold liquid is added. Cream or yoghurt does not need to be heated before adding to the pot.

Stock: The best liquid to use in your potjiekos is home-made stock made with meat, fish or chicken. Have a small potjie at hand in which to make it. Carrot scrapings, green tops and skins of onions, celery leaves and vegetable peels can all be placed in a potjie. Cover with cold water, add fresh herbs and seasonings, such as bay leaves and cloves, and simmer slowly to draw out the flavour.

Wine: Both red and white wine can be used in potjiekos with delicious results, giving depth and richness to the flavours of food. Generally, white wine is used with white meats, seafood and chicken, and red wine with darker meats, such as beef, lamb, duck and venison. Wine will sometimes react with the metal of the potjie and this will give the dish an unpleasant taste. Food cooked in wine should never be left in the potjie for too long. The same applies to dishes containing vinegar.

The Fire

There is no doubt that potjiekos should be cooked over a proper wood fire, and preferably not a fire made with any of the commercial charcoal products that are on the market today. Any kind of firewood can be used; unlike a braai, the choice of firewood does not affect the taste of the meat. A long-burning wood, such as hardekool, vine stumps, camel thorn, umbrella thorn and sickle bush, or mealie husks, is the most convenient. It is important, however, that the wood is dry and that you have enough to last for the entire cooking process, which can last from 2–4 hours, and sometimes longer.

There is an art to knowing exactly when the fire is ready. The fire should be quite hot to thoroughly heat the pot and brown the meat, but thereafter you need only the occasional log or couple of coals to keep the food simmering slowly. It will be perfect for simmering when you are able to hold your hand just above the coals. It's a good idea to keep a separate fire going to one side in case you need more coals.

The Pot

A three-legged cast-iron pot with a handle is the most suitable, although a flat-bottomed cast-iron pot with a tightly fitting lid can be used instead provided it is placed on bricks or a sturdy metal tripod over an open fire. Usually, though, a flat-bottomed pot is used for the making of bread since its shape makes the removal of the bread much easier.

TREATING THE POT

Before the ritual of cooking can begin, however, the potjie must first be seasoned. Of course, today there is a new, specially treated and rustproofed potjie on the market, that can be used immediately without any fuss or bother.

However, if it's an old-fashioned potjie, it will have to be 'broken in' in much the same way you would 'break in' a young horse, otherwise your potjiekos will forever taste of rust and iron.

The first step is to fill the pot with water and add discarded vegetables, peels, scrapings and outer leaves and boil all this for as long as possible. Discard the water and peelings, then fill the potjie with the same kind of ingredients and simmer in the oven, on the stove or preferably over an open fire. Repeat this process 4–5 times. Another method is to boil a mixture of vinegar and water in the pot. This process must be repeated several times.

The only thing left to be done is to scour the pot with wood ash and lots of elbow grease. A few scouring sessions will work wonders. Wash the pot after scouring with warm, soapy water and then rinse with clean, cold water and dry thoroughly.

STORING YOUR POTJIE

There is much debate on this aspect amongst the experts. Some believe a potjie should be greased well with a layer of cooking oil or fat, while others think it should be stored as it is. If a little rust forms it can easily be removed just before use with wood ash or fine steel wool.

The following bit of practical advice was given to me by a good friend. Crumple some newspaper and stuff it into the potjie's belly. The newspaper will absorb any odours and the pot won't rust. An added advantage is that the newspaper will come in handy later when building the fire.

Guidelines for a Perfect Potjie

Some experts believe that the meat should first be browned in a little cooking oil or butter and cooking oil in the potjie. A meat cut with a thick layer of fat, such as brisket, may be browned in its own fat. Browning the meat improves the flavour and colour of the meat and helps seal in the juices. However, if the meat has been marinated in yoghurt or buttermilk, it isn't practical to wipe off the marinade in order to brown the meat. Remember to brown the meat by adding a few pieces at a time. If you add all the meat at once, the pot will cool off too quickly, a loss of meat juices will take place and the meat will boil rather than brown. Once the meat has browned, add chopped onion and stir until it is transparent, then add heated stock.

Meat takes longer to cook than vegetables, so simmer the meat until it is almost tender before placing the vegetables on top of it. Arrange the vegetables in layers, beginning with the ones that take longest to cook, such as potatoes and carrots.

Only a little liquid is necessary, since the pot's heavy, tight-fitting lid and round fat-bellied shape will cause condensation of the steam into moisture and provide more than enough liquid. Don't lift the lid too often as this results in extensive evaporation and delays the cooking process.

A thinner, natural gravy is more appetizing than a thick, glutinous one. However, if you prefer a thicker meat gravy, add a couple of potatoes at the beginning of the cooking process and simmer until soft. Mash one or two of the potatoes to thicken the gravy. Another method of thickening the liquid is by removing the lid and increasing the heat slightly to allow the liquid to boil rapidly, thus reducing it.

It is important not to stir the potjiekos during the cooking process. Give it a quick stir at the beginning when the meat is browning and the onions are being sautéed. An exception to this rule is an offal potjie. If the tripe and trotters are not stirred, they will burn so badly that you will have to discard the entire contents of your potjie and be forced to serve canned food instead. Use a stick for stirring, because a spoon tends to break up the food, which you have so carefully tried to keep in solid, recognizable pieces.

Beef

Beef shin
and three bean potjie

Potjie Nos. 2 and 3

250 g kidney beans
250 g haricot beans
1 litre cold water
15 ml cooking or olive oil
1.5 kg beef shin, sawn into thick slices
250 g pork belly, cut into pieces (keep rind on)
1 medium onion, chopped
1 x 410 g can tomatoes, chopped
500 ml beef stock
10–15 ml salt
1 ml peri-peri or small piece of chilli
250 g green beans
2 large frankfurters

Rinse dried beans thoroughly under cold water. Place in a No. 2 potjie, cover with 1 litre cold water and bring slowly to the boil. Boil rapidly for 5 minutes. Remove from heat, leave lid on and allow to soak for 1 hour.

Heat oil in a No. 3 potjie. Add meat and brown. Add onion and sauté lightly until golden brown and transparent. Drain beans and place on top of meat. Heat tomatoes, stock, salt and peri-peri or chilli and add to meat. Cover with lid and simmer for 2–2$^1/_2$ hours or until meat is almost tender. Top and tail green beans, place on top of meat. Cut frankfurters into thick slices and place on top of beans. Cover and simmer for 12–15 minutes or until green beans are just cooked but still crisp and the sausages heated through. Stir gently. This is a one-pot meal and does not require any side dishes.

Serves 8–10

Beef shin and three bean potjie

Topside pot roast
Potjie No. 4

2.5–3 kg topside (in one piece)
2 cloves garlic, slivered
30 ml butter
30 ml cooking oil
2 large onions, cut into rings
1 green pepper, seeded and
    cut into strips
1 beef stock cube
250 ml dry red wine
250 ml boiling water
12 medium potatoes
1 large or 2 small butternuts
10 small carrots
1 kg green beans
1 sprig fresh rosemary or
    5 ml dried
5 ml salt
freshly ground black pepper
    to taste
12 button mushrooms
    (optional)
½ packet rich oxtail soup
    powder

Make small incisions in meat and insert slivers of garlic. Heat butter and oil in a potjie over medium heat. Place meat in pot and brown on all sides. Add onion rings and green pepper and sauté until golden and transparent (not brown). Heat stock cube, red wine and boiling water in a smaller pot and add to meat. Reduce heat, cover pot and allow to simmer for 1½–2 hours or until meat is almost tender.

Prepare vegetables while pot is simmering. Scrub potatoes and butternut, but do not peel. Halve potatoes and cut butternut into portions, after removing seeds. Leave potato and butternut in cold water until required. Scrub carrots and top and tail green beans and set aside. Check liquid in potjie after 1½ hours. Add more boiling water if necessary. Season meat with rosemary, salt and pepper.

When meat is almost tender, add potatoes and butternut. Allow to simmer for 30 minutes. Arrange carrots, beans and mushrooms, if using, in layers on top of meat and allow to simmer for another 15 minutes. Mix packet soup to a paste with cold water (see instructions on packet) and add to meat to thicken gravy. Allow to simmer for another 10–15 minutes. Use a fork to test whether potatoes and butternut are done. To test whether meat is tender, pull off a strand of meat with your fingers. Remove meat from pot and place on a carving board. Slice thinly and serve with the vegetables and gravy. Serve with crusty home-made bread or Potbrood (page 84).
Serves 12–14

Beef, bacon and mushroom potjie
Potjie No. 4

750 g bacon, rinds removed
2 onions, sliced
1 kg mushrooms, sliced
15 ml cooking oil
4 kg chuck, cubed
1 kg baby carrots
1 kg baby potatoes
1.5 kg green beans
50 ml chopped parsley
500 g tomatoes, skinned and
    chopped

Cut bacon into pieces and fry in potjie until crisp. Add onion and mushrooms and sauté until onion is transparent. Remove from potjie and set aside. Add oil to potjie, add meat gradually and brown. Layer the meat, onion and mushroom mixture, carrots, potatoes and beans in the potjie. Sprinkle with chopped parsley and place tomatoes on top. Cover with lid and simmer slowly for 1½–2 hours or until meat is tender. Serve with rice and stewed peaches.
Serves 12

Curried beef with stampkoring
Potjie No. 2 or 3

1 kg beef neck or flat rib,
    sawn into portions
15 ml cooking oil
2 onions, chopped
1 clove garlic, chopped
15 ml chopped root ginger or
    5 ml ground ginger
15 ml medium curry powder
small piece of chilli
5 ml turmeric
5 ml ground coriander
1 stick cinnamon
1 bay leaf
5 ml salt
15 ml tomato paste
250 ml beef stock
250 ml hanepoot wine
250 ml uncooked stampkoring
    (pearl wheat)

Heat oil, add meat a little at a time and brown on all sides, stirring occasionally. Add onion and garlic and sauté until golden brown and transparent. Add ginger, curry powder, chilli, remaining spices, bay leaf and salt. Stir thoroughly until well mixed. Heat tomato paste, stock and wine and add to meat. Cover with lid and simmer for 1½–2 hours or until meat is almost tender. Add stampkoring in a thin layer on top of meat. Replace lid and simmer a further 30–40 minutes or until liquid has been absorbed and the meat and stampkoring are tender. Serve with onion sambal, cucumber sambal (page 62) and chutney.
Serves 6–8

Variation
Use samp, brown rice or barley instead of stampkoring.

Oxtail and trotter potjie

Oxtail and Trotter potjie
Potjie No. 3

The oxtail and pig's trotter is an unusual and delicious combination.

1 oxtail, jointed
1 pig's trotter, sawn into slices
30 ml cooking oil
2 onions, sliced
2 cloves garlic, crushed
2 leeks, cut into rings
10 ml salt
freshly ground black pepper to taste
50 ml chopped parsley
1 bay leaf
1 x 410 g can tomatoes, coarsely chopped
250 ml dry white wine
250 ml uncooked stampkoring, brown rice or barley

Brown meat in heated cooking oil. Add onion, garlic and leeks and sauté lightly until golden brown and transparent. Add salt, pepper, parsley and bay leaf. Stir well. Heat tomatoes and wine, pour over meat and cover with lid. Allow to simmer over low heat for about 3–4 hours until meat is tender. Spoon a thin layer of stampkoring on top of meat. Cover with lid and simmer for a further 30 minutes or until stampkoring is tender.
Serves 6–8

Curried flat rib and fruit pot
Potjie No.3

The combination of fruit and meat is not only a unique combination, but is characteristic of South African cuisine. The addition of desiccated coconut, instead of cake flour, adds to the flavour while serving as a thickening agent.

1.5 kg flat rib, sawn into
  portions
15 ml cooking oil
1 large onion, cut into rings
2 cloves garlic, crushed
30 ml chopped root ginger
20 ml medium curry powder
1 bay leaf
1 stick cinnamon
2 ml turmeric
500–750 ml hot beef stock
125 ml desiccated coconut
30 ml wine vinegar
1 green apple, cut into
  wedges
2 bananas, peeled and sliced
75 g sultanas
75 g dried apricots
10 ml salt

Heat oil in potjie and brown meat. Add onion and garlic and sauté until golden brown and transparent. Add ginger, curry powder, bay leaf, cinnamon and turmeric and sauté for a few minutes. Add hot stock and remaining ingredients. Cover and allow to simmer for 1¹/₂–2 hours or until meal is tender. Serve with rice or Stampkoring (page 79) and Tomato sambal (page 79).
Serves 6

Onion pot roast
Potjie No. 3

1.5–2 kg aitchbone
2 cloves garlic, slivered
125 g spek, cut into strips
30 ml cooking oil
500 g pickling onions, peeled
150 ml dry red wine
5–7 ml salt
freshly ground black pepper
  to taste
15 ml tomato paste
1 bay leaf
1 brinjal, cut into rings
2 leeks, washed and sliced
2 green peppers, seeded and
  quartered
1 pimiento, seeded and
  quartered

Lard meat with garlic and strips of spek. (This should preferably be done in the kitchen as it is difficult to handle spek once it gets too warm.) Brown meat in heated cooking oil. Cut a cross in the base of each onion to prevent it from breaking up during cooking. Add onions to meat and sauté. Heat red wine, salt, pepper, tomato paste and bay leaf and add to meat and onions. Cover and simmer for 1¹/₂–2 hours or until meat is almost tender. Add brinjal, leeks, peppers and pimiento to meat and simmer for 10 minutes or until vegetables are cooked but still crisp.
Serves 6–8

> Variation
> Substitute half meat stock and half wine vinegar for the red wine.

Pichelsteiner potjie
Potjie No 4

This recipe is based on the famous German dish 'Eintopf' or 'Pichelsteiner Fleisch'. The meat has been kept in large cuts and carved after cooking. An advantage is that this dish can also be served cold.

1.5 kg boneless point brisket
2 pickled pork shanks
  (Eisbein)
1 corned ox tongue
1.5 kg aitchbone, larded with
  about 100 g strips of spek,
  carrot strips and celery
  stalks
1 onion
2 cloves garlic, crushed
6 stalks celery, cut into
  100 mm lengths
6 carrots
2 bay leaves
6 black peppercorns
1 whole allspice
500 g smoked sausage

Place meat and vegetables in the potjie. Tie spices in a muslin bag and add to potjie. Cover with cold water and bring slowly to the boil. Allow to simmer for 2–2¹/₂ hours or until meat is tender. Make incisions in sausage to prevent it from splitting and add to potjie. Allow to simmer for a further 30 minutes. Arrange meat on a large platter, slice and serve with Herbed mustard sauce (page 78) and Potbrood (page 84).
Serves 12

Curried flat rib and fruit pot

Oxtail with dumplings
Potjie No. 3

1 oxtail, jointed
15 ml cooking oil
1 onion, chopped
1 clove garlic, chopped
2 bay leaves
1 sprig fresh rosemary
    or 5 ml dried
1 sprig parsley or 5 ml dried
500 ml beef stock
30 ml vinegar or lemon juice
10 ml salt
freshly ground black pepper
    to taste
4 leeks, cut into chunks
2 stalks leafy celery,
    cut into pieces
6 baby carrots, scrubbed
250 ml green peas
    (fresh or frozen)

DUMPLINGS
250 ml cake flour
5 ml baking powder
2 ml salt
60 g butter
cold water or soda water
    to mix dough

Heat oil and brown oxtail. Add onion and garlic and sauté until golden brown. Add bay leaves, rosemary, parsley, hot stock and vinegar or lemon juice. Season meat with salt and pepper. Cover with lid and simmer for 3–4 hours or until meat is tender. Layer vegetables on top of meat, starting with leeks and celery, then carrots and peas. Add more stock if necessary.

For the dumplings, sift dry ingredients together and rub in butter until the mixture resembles fine breadcrumbs. Add enough cold water or soda water to make a soft dough. Place spoonfuls of dough on top of meat and vegetables. Replace lid and simmer for 30 minutes. Don't lift the lid or the dumplings will collapse.
Serves 4–6

Bacchus beef potjie
Potjie No. 3

Dessert wines like muscadel or hanepoot are seldom used in meat cookery. However, I have discovered that, instead of the customary pinch of sugar when preparing dishes containing a fair amount of tomato, the addition of a little of this wine makes a delicious difference.

1 kg thin flank, cubed
30 ml cooking oil
1 onion, chopped
1 clove garlic, crushed
1 x 410 g can tomatoes,
    coarsely chopped
10 ml salt
freshly ground back pepper
    to taste
30 ml chopped fresh basil or
    10 ml dried
150 ml hanepoot or white
    muscadel wine
30 ml lemon juice
15 ml cake flour
30 ml chopped fresh parsley
    or 10 ml dried

Heat oil and brown meat. Add onion and garlic and sauté until golden brown and transparent. Add tomatoes, salt, pepper and basil. Heat wine and add. Season with lemon juice. Cover potjie with lid and allow to simmer for 1½–2 hours or until meat is tender. Mix flour with a little cold water to form a paste. Add to meat. Simmer for a few minutes to thicken. Just before serving, sprinkle with parsley and serve with rice, Stampkoring (page 79) or Stywepap (page 77).
Serves 6

Beef and vegetable potjie
Potjie No. 4

1 kg bolo, shin or neck
15 ml cooking oil
5 ml salt
freshly ground black pepper
    to taste
1 clove garlic, crushed
2 onions, coarsely chopped
3 carrots, sliced
300 g cauliflower florets
4 baby marrows, sliced
15 ml brown sugar
100 ml orange juice
125 ml grated Cheddar
    cheese

Cube or slice meat. Heat oil in potjie and brown meat, then season with salt and pepper. Add garlic and onion and sauté until onion is transparent. Add vegetables, brown sugar and orange juice. Cover and simmer for 1½–2 hours or until meat is tender. Just before serving, sprinkle with grated cheese. Serve with baked potatoes.
Serves 6

Brisket with braai sauce

Potjie Nos. 1 and 3

Brisket, like other cuts from the forequarter, makes a particular tasty potjie.

1.5 kg brisket, sawn into slices
15 ml cooking oil

BRAAI SAUCE
2 large onions, chopped
2 cloves garlic, crushed
15 ml cooking oil
1 x 410 g can tomatoes,
   coarsely chopped or
    500 g fresh tomatoes,
   skinned and chopped
125 ml water or meat stock
125 ml brown vinegar
2 ml grated nutmeg
1 ml ground ginger
5 ml paprika
2 whole cloves
2 bay leaves
15 ml Worcestershire sauce
15 ml brown sugar
5 ml salt
30 ml chutney
2 stalks celery, sliced

Prepare braai sauce in a separate small potjie. Sauté onion and garlic in heated oil until light brown and transparent.

Add remaining sauce ingredients. Cover with lid and allow to simmer for 30–45 minutes so that the flavours can combine and the sauce thickens.

Heat oil in a No. 3 potjie until very hot. Add meat a little at a time, stirring so that the meat browns on all sides. Now add braai sauce to meat. Cover with lid and allow to simmer slowly for 2–2¹/₂ hours, or until meat is tender. Serve with Stywepap (page 77) or rice.
Serves 6

Beef and kidney with parsley dumplings

Potjie No. 3

250 g sheep's kidneys
500 g boneless chuck, cubed
15 ml butter
15 ml cooking oil
2 onions, chopped
250 g carrots, diced
500 ml meat stock
30 ml tomato purée
5 ml mixed dried herbs or
   15 ml chopped fresh herbs
10 ml salt
freshly ground black pepper
   to taste

PARSLEY DUMPLINGS
375 ml self-raising flour
3 ml salt
30 ml chopped fresh parsley
60 ml grated butter
iced water

Prepare meat: Halve kidneys and remove outer membrane and core. Heat oil and butter in potjie. Add meat a little at a time and brown on all sides. Add onion and sauté until golden brown and transparent. Add carrots and sauté for 3 minutes. Heat remaining ingredients and add to meat. Cover with lid and allow to simmer for 1¹/₂–2 hours or until meat is tender.

For the dumplings, mix flour, salt and parsley in a bowl. Rub in butter until mixture resembles breadcrumbs. Add enough iced water to form a soft scone-like dough. Knead lightly and shape into 4–8 dumplings. Remove lid, arrange dumplings on top of meat and replace lid. Simmer for a further 20–30 minutes without lifting the lid, otherwise the dumplings will collapse.
Serves 6

Old-fashioned bean soup

Potjie No. 3 or 4

1 kg dried beans (kidney,
   haricot or sugar beans)
1 pickled and smoked pork
   shank
3 litres meat stock
2 large onions, chopped
1 large carrot, diced
1 stalk leafy celery, chopped
1 bay leaf
1 sprig fresh thyme
   or 5 ml dried
10 ml salt
freshly ground black pepper
   to taste
15 ml vinegar or lemon juice
250 g bacon, rinds removed
   and coarsely chopped
30 ml chopped fresh parsley
   or 10 ml dried

Soak beans overnight in enough water to cover. Place pork shank and drained beans in potjie and add enough stock to cover. Bring to the boil, frequently skimming off foam, and simmer until the beans and meat are almost tender. Add vegetables, bay leaf, thyme, salt and pepper and simmer for another 20 minutes or until vegetables are tender. Add vinegar or lemon juice and season soup with more salt and pepper if necessary. Fry bacon until crisp in separate small potjie. Serve soup in suitable deep bowls and sprinkle with a little parsley and bacon.
Serves 6

Variations
Use split peas or lentils instead of beans.
Substitute pork shank for lamb shank and beans for samp.
If pork shank is unobtainable, use bacon rinds or a piece of pork rind.

Special Saturday potjie

Potjie Nos. 1 and 3

A meal in itself.

1 kg boneless chuck, bolo or
   thin flank, cubed
15 ml cooking oil
2 onions, chopped
2 cloves garlic, chopped
2 stalks celery, chopped
2 bay leaves
15 ml chopped fresh oregano
   or 5 ml dried
5 ml scorched ground
   coriander
5 ml ground cumin
7 ml salt
freshly ground black pepper
   to taste
500 ml meat stock
4 medium-sized carrots,
   quartered or 10 small
   carrots
2 large cobs of sweetcorn, cut
   into 25 mm slices or 6 baby
   mealies
1 small Chinese or ordinary
   white cabbage
15 ml cake flour
15 ml soft butter

Heat the oil in a No. 3 potjie. Add meat a little at a time and brown. Add onion, garlic and celery to meat and sauté lightly until golden brown and transparent. Heat herbs, spices and stock in a No. 1 potjie. Pour into No. 3 potjie, cover and allow to simmer for about 2 hours or until meat is tender. Skim off excess fat. Arrange carrots, sweetcorn or mealies and cabbage in layers on top of meat. Replace lid and allow to simmer for 20 minutes. Remove bay leaves and season with more salt and pepper if necessary. Mix flour and butter to a paste and carefully stir into potjie to thicken gravy.
Serves 6

Herbed cheese potbrood

Flat-bottomed Potjie No. 4 or 5

10 ml sugar
300 ml lukewarm water
10 ml dried yeast
750 ml cake flour
125 ml milk powder
15 ml salt
250 ml whole-wheat flour
250 ml grated Cheddar cheese
30 ml snipped chives (optional)
1 clove garlic, chopped (optional)
15 ml chopped fresh herbs or
   5 ml dried mixed herbs
30 ml cooking oil
paprika for dusting top

Dissolve sugar in the lukewarm water. Sprinkle in the dried yeast and set aside for about 10 minutes until the mixture becomes foamy. Sift the cake flour, milk powder and salt together. Add whole-wheat flour, cheese (reserve 30 ml), chives and garlic if using, and herbs and mix lightly. Add oil to flour mixture and stir in lightly. Stir in yeast mixture and blend to a soft almost batter-like dough. Spoon the dough into a well-greased flat-bottomed pot. Brush inside of lid with butter or oil and cover pot. Stand pot in a warm place for dough to rise until doubled in size (about 45 minutes). Sprinkle remaining cheese and paprika on top of the dough. Make a little heap of well-burnt coals and then scrape a hollow in the middle. Place pot in this hollow. Put a few coals on the lid. Bake for 1 hour or until the bread sounds hollow when tapped on the underside with knuckles.
Makes 1 loaf

From left to right: Old-fashioned bean soup (page 15), Herbed cheese potbrood, Rolypoly pudding, Cape winepot, Special Saturday potjie

Winter Warmers

Cape winepot
Potjie No. 1

1 x 750 ml bottle dry red wine
1 orange studded with whole
   cloves
2 sticks cinnamon
6 cardamom pods, bruised
2 stars anise
6 black peppercorns, slightly
   bruised
1 piece naartjie peel

Place wine in potjie. Add orange. Place spices into muslin bag and add to the wine with naartjie peel. Slowly bring wine to the boil. (Remember, the slower the wine is heated, the better the flavour.) Remove from heat. Place a metal spoon into a glass when pouring in the hot wine, otherwise the glass might break.
Serves 3

Rolypoly pudding for the pot
Flat-bottomed Potjie No. 4

SYRUP
375 ml boiling water
250 ml sugar
30 g butter

DOUGH
500 ml cake flour
10 ml baking powder
2 ml salt
110 g butter
2 eggs
60–75 ml milk
smooth apricot jam

To prepare syrup: Mix boiling water and sugar in pot. Stir over low heat until sugar is dissolved. Do not allow syrup to boil before sugar is dissolved. Simmer for about 3 minutes. Stir in butter.

To prepare dough: Sift flour, baking powder and salt together. Cut butter into small pieces and rub lightly into dry ingredients until it resembles fine breadcrumbs. Beat eggs and milk together and add to flour mixture. Blend to a manageable dough that can be easily rolled out. Refrigerate for 30 minutes and then lightly roll out to 5 mm thickness. Spread dough thinly with apricot jam. Roll up and place gently into the simmering syrup. Cover with lid and simmer slowly for 30 minutes or until the pudding is cooked.
Serves 6

Mince

Baked mince and brinjal
Potjie Nos. 2 and 3

2 medium brinjals
30 ml cooking oil
3 medium onions, chopped
2 cloves garlic, chopped
1 kg minced mutton
1 bay leaf
15 ml fresh oregano or 5 ml dried
10 ml salt
freshly ground black pepper to taste
50 ml chopped fresh parsley
1 x 410 g can tomatoes, chopped
50 ml tomato paste
125 ml dry red wine
1 x 410 g can cream of mushroom soup
250 ml meat stock
75 ml grated Parmesan cheese

Cut brinjal into 10 mm slices, sprinkle with salt and allow to stand for 30 minutes. Rinse well in cold water and dry. Brush oil over slices and braai over glowing coals until brown on both sides. Sauté onion and garlic in remaining oil in smaller potjie. Add meat and fry until it changes colour. Add seasonings, tomatoes, tomato paste and wine. Simmer for 30 minutes.

Starting with brinjal, arrange brinjal and meat in layers in larger pot ending with a layer of brinjal.

Mix soup with stock in smaller pot and simmer slowly until mixture is thick. Spoon over meat and brinjal. Sprinkle with cheese. Cover with lid and place a few small coals on lid for a golden-brown top. Simmer slowly for 30–45 minutes or until brinjal is tender.
Serves 8

From left to right: Stuffed cabbage (page 20), Baked mince and brinjal

Potjie meat loaf
Potjie No. 3

1 thick slice bread, crust
    removed
125 ml port
800 g lean minced beef
1 egg, beaten
2 ml ground cinnamon
1 ml ground coriander
2 cloves garlic, chopped
30 ml finely chopped fresh
    parsley
15 ml butter
barbecue spice to taste
garlic salt to taste
freshly ground black pepper
    to taste
10 ml lemon juice
125 ml meat stock
4 tomatoes, skinned and
    thickly sliced

Soak bread in port. Mix meat, egg, cinnamon, coriander, garlic and parsley. Add soaked bread and 5 ml melted butter and mix thoroughly. Use remaining butter to butter base of potjie. Place meat in pot and press firmly into the shape of a loaf. Sprinkle with barbecue spice, garlic salt, freshly ground black pepper and lemon juice. Pour heated stock over meat, cover with lid and simmer slowly over medium coals for 30 minutes. Arrange tomatoes on top of meat and simmer for another 30 minutes. Serve with rice and a green salad.
Serves 6

Stuffed cabbage
Potjie No. 1 or 2

1 medium cabbage
1 onion, chopped
1 clove garlic, chopped
15 ml cooking oil
500 g minced meat
5 ml salt
freshly ground black pepper
    to taste
15 ml tomato paste
50 ml chopped fresh parsley
350 ml meat stock
15 ml wine vinegar
125 ml fresh breadcrumbs
150 ml grated Cheddar cheese

The pot should be large enough for the cabbage to fit in snugly.

Discard limp and blemished outside leaves of cabbage and cut the top off level. This piece forms the 'lid'. Hollow out the inside carefully without damaging the sides.

For the filling, sauté onion and garlic in heated cooking oil until transparent. Add meat and sauté until it changes colour. Add seasoning, tomato paste, parsley and 100 ml stock. Allow filling to cool off slightly, then spoon into hollowed out cabbage. Replace 'lid' and tie cabbage with string to hold it together.

Grease the pot with butter. Mix remaining stock and vinegar and pour over cabbage. Sprinkle with breadcrumbs and cheese and cover pot. Simmer slowly for 20–30 minutes or until the cabbage is tender. Remove string and serve.
Serves 6

Ou vrou onder die kombers 1
Flat-bottomed potjie No. 3

This traditional old recipe is typical of those from the Karoo, Namibia and the Kalahari. Originally mutton was used, but beef can just as easily be substituted.

500 g minced beef
1 onion, chopped
15 ml melted mutton fat,
    or 15 ml cooking oil
15 ml vinegar
5 ml salt
freshly ground black pepper
    to taste
2 ml ground cloves
2 ml ground coriander
grated nutmeg to taste

BATTER
250 ml cake flour
2 ml salt
5 ml baking powder
2 eggs, beaten
375 ml water, or milk and water
125 ml melted butter or
    melted mutton fat or lard

To prepare meat, sauté meat and onion in 15 ml melted mutton fat or cooking oil until the meat changes colour. Add vinegar, salt, pepper and spices and stir lightly. Using the back of a spoon, press meat mixture onto the bottom of the pot.

To make the batter, sift flour, salt and baking powder together. Beat eggs into water or milk and water and add to dry ingredients. Stir well. Stir in melted butter or fat, then pour batter over meat. The batter should be thin enough to soak in between the meat. Cover and bake slowly over a small fire for 30–40 minutes or until the mixture is cooked. If a golden-brown crust is desired, place a few small coals on top of the lid.
Serves 6

Cabbage frikkadels
Potjie No. 3

8 or more large cabbage leaves
home-made tomato sauce
   (page 66)

STUFFING
15 ml butter
15 ml cooking oil
500 g minced beef,
   mutton or pork
1 medium onion, finely chopped
1 slice white bread, soaked in
   125 ml milk or meat stock
30 ml sultanas or seedless
   raisins
pinch of dried mixed herbs
30 ml chopped fresh parsley
   or 10 ml dried
5 ml salt
freshly ground black pepper
   to taste

First make the stuffing: Heat butter and oil in pot. Add meat and onion and fry lightly until meat changes colour. Mash bread with a fork. Mix meat, bread and remaining stuffing ingredients together and allow to cool.

   Pour boiling water over cabbage leaves. Drain. Place leaves on a wooden board and flatten gently by hand. Spoon a little stuffing into the centre of the leaf. Fold the leaf over and place into pot with fold underneath or close with a toothpick. Pour home-made tomato sauce over. Cover and simmer slowly for 20–30 minutes.
Serves 6

Variation
Sprinkle a little grated Cheddar cheese over the frikkadels. Place a few small coals on top of the lid to make sure that the cheese melts quickly and cooks to a golden-brown colour.

Hint
Prepare the tomato sauce in advance and store it in the refrigerator or freezer until needed.

Frikkadels with red cabbage
Flat-bottomed potjie No. 3

500 g finely minced beef
1 slice white bread, crumbled
1 small onion, finely chopped
5 ml salt
freshly ground black pepper
   to taste
1 ml grated nutmeg
200 ml soda water
30 ml butter
30 ml cooking oil
½ red cabbage, shredded
   (about 500 g)
1 green apple, sliced
30 ml white wine vinegar
15 ml red currant jelly or
   smooth apricot jam
100 ml meat stock

Mix mince, breadcrumbs, onion, salt, pepper, nutmeg and soda water together. Shape into frikkadels. Stand in a cool place for about 30 minutes to firm up. Heat butter and oil in pot and brown frikkadels. Remove from pot and set aside. Sauté cabbage in pan juices. Add apple and sauté for a few minutes. Add remaining ingredients and simmer for a few minutes. Arrange frikkadels on top of cabbage. Cover with lid and simmer slowly for 20–30 minutes or until frikkadels are cooked.
Serves 6

Pineapple and rice mince
Potjie No. 3

500 g coarsely minced pork
30 ml cooking oil
1 onion, chopped
1 green pepper, seeded and
   chopped
250 ml uncooked rice
375 ml fresh or frozen corn
   kernels
250 ml fresh or frozen peas
1 fresh pineapple, diced
1 tomato, skinned and
   chopped
15 ml soy sauce
50 ml fruit chutney
500 ml meat or chicken stock

Heat oil in pot. Add meat, onion and green pepper and sauté until meat has changed colour and onion is transparent. Remove half the meat and set aside. Spoon half the rice on top of meat and then arrange the corn, peas and pineapple in layers on top, ending with a layer each of the remaining rice and meat. Spoon tomato on top. Heat soy sauce, chutney and stock and pour over. Cover with lid and simmer for 45–60 minutes or until most of the stock has been absorbed. The mixture should not be dry though, but fairly moist.
Serves 6

Curried potjie rolypoly

Potjie No. 1 and Flat-bottomed
Potjie No. 3

STUFFING

15 ml cooking oil
1 onion, chopped
2 cloves garlic, chopped
15 ml medium curry powder
2 ml salt
500 g minced meat
1 small green apple, grated
  or chopped
15 ml wine vinegar
15 ml fruit chutney

PASTRY

500 ml cake flour
5 ml salt
30 ml butter
cold water to mix pastry

CURRY SAUCE

15 ml cooking oil
1 onion, chopped
5 ml medium curry powder
2 ml turmeric
250 ml meat stock
2 ml salt
1 ml grated nutmeg
1 bay leaf or lemon leaf
15 ml fruit chutney
15 ml vinegar or lemon juice

For the stuffing, place cooking oil in the round-bellied pot and heat. Add onion and garlic and sauté until transparent. Add curry powder and salt and fry for a few minutes. Add remaining stuffing ingredients and sauté for 5 minutes, using a fork to break up any lumps in the mince. Remove from the potjie and leave in a cool place until cold.

For the pastry, sift the dry ingredients together. Cut butter into smaller pieces and rub into the flour until the mixture resembles fine breadcrumbs. Make a well in the centre of the flour and add enough cold water to form a stiff dough. Roll out the dough into a 10 mm thick rectangle. Spread chilled stuffing on the inside of the pastry, leaving 25 mm clear around the edges to prevent the stuffing from falling out during cooking. Roll up the pastry like a Swiss roll. Brush the edges with a little cold water to secure. Wrap meat roll in a damp cloth, then with plastic wrap. Keep in a cool place while preparing sauce.

For the sauce, place oil in the flat-bottomed potjie. Add onion and sauté until transparent. Add curry powder and fry for 2 minutes. Add remaining sauce ingredients and simmer for another 5 minutes. Gently place the unwrapped, chilled meat roll in the sauce. Cover with lid and simmer over a small fire for 30–40 minutes or until pastry is cooked. Serve with bananas left in their skins and baked in the coals.
Serves 6

Curried potjie rolypoly

Offal

Curried pens and pootjies
Potjie No. 4 or 5

A prize winning recipe in the Sarie-Kellerprinz potjie competition. You need to start very early as this traditional dish of tripe and trotters requires long, slow simmering to become soft and flavoursome.

4 lamb's tripe and trotters
3 kg saddle of lamb chops
50 ml blanc de noir wine
salt to taste
3–4 peppercorns
5 medium onions, quartered
25 medium potatoes
20 ml curry powder
20 ml turmeric
50 ml white sugar
50 ml white vinegar

Wash tripe and trotters thoroughly. Cut tripe into 25 mm pieces and simmer in a little water in the potjie for 1 hour. Add trotters and chops, wine, salt and peppercorns. Simmer slowly for about 6 hours so that the tripe and trotters become soft and gelatinous. Make sure the meat does not dry out and add more water when necessary. When offal is tender, add onions and potatoes. Mix curry powder, turmeric, sugar, salt and vinegar together and add to the potjie. Simmer for a further 40–45 minutes, adding water if necessary to avoid burning. Serve with Potbrood (page 84), Stampkoring (page 79) or rice, and stewed peaches.
Serves 20

Curried pens and pootjies

Kidneys in red wine
Potjie No. 1

6 sheep's kidneys
    or 2 ox kidneys
6 rashers bacon, rind removed
    and coarsely chopped
15 ml butter
1 onion, chopped
30 ml chopped fresh parsley
    or 10 ml dried
15 ml chopped fresh thyme or
    5 ml dried
5 ml salt
freshly ground black pepper
    to taste
125 ml dry red wine
125 ml meat stock

Remove outside skin from kidneys. If the kidneys are fresh it will be easy to pull off, otherwise it will have to be soaked in milk or lukewarm salted water for a few minutes. Cut kidneys in half and remove the hard core. Cut into cubes. Place bacon in potjie and fry until crisp. Add butter and when heated add kidneys and sauté until lightly browned. Add onion and sauté until transparent. Heat remaining ingredients and add to kidneys. Cover with lid and simmer for 30 minutes or until kidneys are tender. Ox kidneys will take a little longer to cook. Serve with Roosterkoek (page 83). Cut roosterkoek in half lengthways, three quarters of the way through, and spoon kidney mixture into the centre.
Serves 3–4

Ou vrou onder die kombers 2
Potjie No. 2 or 3

As a child, this dish often appeared on our menus, especially on Fridays. As Friday was the weekly sheep-slaughtering day, the caul was still warm and thus easy to handle, while nothing could beat the flavour of the fresh liver.

500 g sheep's liver
7 ml salt
freshly ground black pepper
    to taste
15 ml wine vinegar or
    lemon juice
1 egg (optional)
1 slice white bread soaked
    in milk or meat stock
5 ml grated lemon rind
10 ml fresh thyme or 5 ml dried
1 piece caul fat

Plunge liver into boiling water for 1 minute. Remove the skin. Shred liver finely with a fork. Add remaining ingredients, except the caul, to the liver and mix well. Place caul on a board and open it up to flatten it, then place at the bottom of the potjie. Spoon liver mixture on top of the caul. Fold sides of the caul over mixture so that it is completely covered. If the caul refuses to lie flat, place a weighted enamel plate on top or fasten it with cocktail sticks. Cover with lid and bake over a slow fire for 45–60 minutes or until the liver is cooked.
Serves 6

Hint
If caul fat is unavailable, rashers of streaky bacon may be used instead. Remove the rind and arrange the rashers so that they overlap on the base of the potjie.

Quick chicken liver and rice potjie
Potjie No. 3

50 g butter
1 large onion, chopped
2 rashers bacon, rind
    removed and chopped
2 x 250 g chicken livers
1 bay leaf
5 ml fresh sage or 2 ml dried
2 ml salt
freshly ground black pepper
    to taste
50 ml dry white wine or
    chicken stock

RICE
1 small onion, chopped
50 g butter
500 ml uncooked rice
5 ml salt
freshly ground black pepper
    to taste
15 ml fresh parsley or 5 ml dried
1 litre warm chicken stock
    (more if necessary)

Heat butter in potjie and sauté onion until transparent. Add bacon and fry for a few minutes. Add cleaned chicken livers and fry lightly. Add bay leaf, sage, salt, pepper and wine or stock and simmer for a few minutes. Remove from potjie and set aside. Wipe the potjie out with paper towelling.

To prepare the rice, sauté onion in heated butter in the same potjie. Add the rice and fry until the rice is well coated with butter. Add salt, pepper and parsley. Stir, then remove half the rice. Spoon half of the liver mixture in a layer on top of the rice. Repeat layers of rice and liver. Pour the warmed stock over the top. Cover with lid and simmer slowly over a very small fire for 30–40 minutes or until the rice is cooked, adding more stock if necessary to ensure the dish is moist and creamy.
Serves 6–8

Sweet-and-sour liver and kidneys
Potjie No. 2

This is one of my favourites that I remember from childhood. Nobody can prepare it as well as old Kwets, who has been part of our family for over 30 years.

1 sheep's liver
2 sheep's kidneys
1 sheep's heart
15 ml butter
15 ml cooking oil
1 onion, sliced
15 ml cake flour
250 ml meat stock
15–30 ml vinegar
5 ml sugar
5 ml salt
freshly ground black pepper
   to taste

Pull off the outside skin of the liver. Cut out the tubes and slice liver into thin strips, or dice. Discard outside skin of kidneys. Cut kidneys in half, remove hard core, and dice. Rinse out heart thoroughly under cold running water, then cut out tubes. Dice heart. Heat butter and oil in potjie, add meat and brown. Add onion and sauté until transparent. Sprinkle flour over meat and stir. Add heated stock, vinegar and sugar and season with salt and pepper. Cover with lid and simmer for 20–30 minutes or until the meat is tender.
Serves 6

Braised ox heart
Potjie Nos. $^3/_4$ and 2 or 3

1 ox heart
250 g flank or breast
   of mutton
15 ml cooking oil
15 ml butter
3 onions, sliced
250 ml meat stock
   or dry white wine
2 ml ground cloves
5 ml ground coriander
1 ml grated nutmeg
1 ml ground allspice
30 ml vinegar

Soak heart in hot salted water for about 30 minutes. Discard hard tubes and cut heart into cubes. Discard outside skin from mutton and cut meat into smaller pieces. Heat oil and butter in larger potjie and brown meat. Remove meat from potjie and set aside. Add more oil and butter to potjie if necessary. Add onion and sauté until transparent. Leave the onion on the bottom of the potjie and spoon meat on top. Heat remaining ingredients in small potjie, pour over meat and cover with lid. Simmer slowly for 1 hour or until meat is tender.
Serves 4

Variations
Substitute red wine or tomato juice for meat stock or white wine.
Place 250 g mixed dried fruit on top of meat and increase liquid if necessary.
Add another 350 ml liquid to the meat and place dumplings (page 14 or 15) on top of meat. Cover with lid and simmer slowly for another 20 minutes without peeping.

Tripe in potjie
Potjie No. 2

1 kg beef tripe
15 ml cooking oil
1 large onion, thinly sliced
1 clove garlic, chopped
3 tomatoes, skinned and
   chopped or 1 x 410 g can
   whole tomatoes, chopped
50 ml chopped fresh parsley
5 ml sugar
10 ml salt
freshly ground black pepper
   to taste
pinch of grated nutmeg
250 ml dry white wine
10 baby or 4 large potatoes,
   quartered

Boil tripe in salted water for $2^1/_2$ hours or until tender. Drain, dry well and cut into strips. Discard salt water and dry potjie thoroughly. Heat cooking oil and sauté onion and garlic until transparent. Add remaining ingredients, except tripe and potatoes, and simmer until the sauce has thickened a little. Add tripe and stir well. Arrange potatoes on top and cover with lid. Simmer slowly for 30–40 minutes or until potatoes are tender.
Serves 4

Hint
The tripe can be prepared ahead of time. Boil tripe as described until tender, then drain. Allow to cool, then place in enough salted water to cover. The salt will act as a preservative, which will ensure that you can keep the tripe unrefrigerated for at least one day.

Lamb

Denningvleis
Potjie No. 2 or 3

This traditional Cape Malay dish used to be known as *Dengdengvleis* on the Batavian *rijstafel*. The original dish was prepared with buffalo meat. *Dengdeng* means meat pickled with salt and flavoured with spices. The meat is then sliced, dried in the sun and fried in coconut oil. Here it is somewhat different. Although it may look like an ordinary lamb stew, it has a lingering oriental flavour.

1 kg breast of lamb, sawn into portions or 1 kg neck slices
15 ml cooking oil
2 large onions, sliced
5 large cloves garlic
5 whole allspice
5 whole cloves
2 bay leaves
1 green chilli, seeded and finely chopped
7 ml salt
freshly ground black pepper to taste
125 ml meat stock
30 ml seedless tamarind
250 ml boiling water
5 ml grated nutmeg

Heat oil in potjie and sauté onion until transparent. Meanwhile, grind garlic, all the spices and chilli to a fine paste with a pestle and mortar. Remove onion and set aside. Brown meat in remaining oil. Place onion on top of meat with the spice paste and season with salt and pepper. Add heated stock. Cover with lid and simmer for 40–50 minutes. Soak tamarind in the boiling water for 15–20 minutes. Drain in a sieve and add tamarind water and nutmeg to meat. Replace lid and simmer for a further 15 minutes. Serve with yellow rice and raisins.
Serves 6

Denningvleis

Lamb and brinjal potjie
Potjie No. 3 or 4

This is based on the southern Italian dish, Ciambotta. Although it originates from Calabria, southern Italy, we can definitely 'borrow' it because it is cooked over an open fire. This dish is unusual in that the meat and vegetables are first browned on the grid.

4 medium brinjals
1 green pepper
1 kg breast of lamb, sawn
   into portions
1 onion, sliced
2 cloves garlic, crushed
30 ml cooking oil
1 x 410 g can whole tomatoes,
   coarsely chopped
50 ml chopped fresh parsley
10 ml salt
freshly ground black pepper
   to taste
1 sprig fresh rosemary
1 sprig fresh thyme
1 bay leaf

Peel brinjal, if preferred, and cut into 10 mm thick slices. Sprinkle with salt and allow to stand for 30 minutes. Rinse under cold water and dry on paper towelling. Braai brinjal and green pepper over coals. Drizzle cooking oil over vegetables at short intervals. Braai meat over coals until brown.

Meanwhile, sauté onion and garlic in a little heated oil. Add tomatoes, parsley, salt, pepper, herbs and bay leaf and simmer until thick, stirring to prevent burning. Place meat, brinjal and green pepper, peeled, seeded and cut into strips, into tomato sauce, cover with lid and simmer for 1 hour or until meat is tender.
Serves 6

Patrick and Beverley's curry potjie
Potjie No. 2

1.5 kg mutton shank, sawn
   into slices
30 ml cooking oil
500 g lamb's kidney
2 large onions, sliced
6 cloves garlic, chopped
1 small piece root ginger,
   peeled and chopped
pinch of ground pimiento
6 whole cloves
6 cardamom seeds, crushed
1 stick cinnamon
2 ml salt
3 bay leaves
a little chopped fresh
   coriander leaves
15 ml garlic and ginger masala
15 ml garam masala
5 ml turmeric
75 ml vinegar
30 ml smooth apricot jam
250 ml semi-sweet wine (stein)
8 baby potatoes, peeled
4 carrots, sliced
250 g green beans, sliced
250 g cauliflower,
   broken into florets
250 ml shredded cabbage
300 g mushrooms,
   wiped and sliced
2 ripe tomatoes,
   skinned and chopped

Brown meat a few pieces at a time in heated cooking oil Add the kidneys and brown with meat. Add onion and garlic and sauté until transparent. Add ginger, pimiento (allspice), cloves, cardamom, cinnamon, salt, bay leaves and coriander leaves. Mix masalas, turmeric, vinegar and jam together and add to meat. Heat wine and pour over meat. Cover with lid and simmer for about 45 minutes.

Layer vegetables on top of meat in the order listed. Spoon tomato over the top, replace the lid and simmer for 45 minutes or until the vegetables are cooked and the tomato has formed a pulp. Serve with rice.
Serves 8

Mrs Brown's lamb curry
Potjie No. 3

4 large onions, sliced
5 ml chopped root ginger
2 cloves garlic, chopped
15 ml cooking oil or ghee
15 ml fresh mixed herbs
   or 5 ml dried
10 ml curry powder
10 ml turmeric
5 ml ground coriander
1 kg neck of lamb, sawn
   into slices
250 ml meat stock
1 tomato, skinned and
   chopped
7 ml salt
5 ml garam masala

Sauté onion, ginger and garlic in heated oil. Add herbs and stir over heat for 2–3 minutes. Add curry powder, turmeric and coriander and fry for 2–3 minutes. Stir continuously to prevent burning. Add meat and the heated stock. Cover with lid and simmer for 1 hour. Add remaining ingredients and simmer for a further 30 minutes or until meat is tender and tomato reduced to pulp. Serve with rice.
Serves 4

Leg of lamb in the potjie
Flat-bottomed Potjie No. 3

2 kg leg of lamb
4 cloves garlic, slivered
15 ml chopped root ginger
4 cardamom pods
5 black peppercorns
5 whole allspice
5 ml ground coriander
1 bay leaf
5 ml grated lemon rind
100 ml lemon juice or
   wine vinegar
15 ml butter
15 ml cooking oil
1 large onion, chopped
200 ml meat stock
50 ml hanepoot or white
   muscadel wine
7 ml salt
125 ml seedless raisins
8 pickling onions
6 medium carrots
3 stalks celery, cut into pieces

Remove gland from leg. Make tiny cuts in the meat and insert garlic. Use a pestle and mortar to grind ginger, cardamom, peppercorns, allspice, coriander, bay leaf and lemon rind into a paste. Mix with lemon juice or vinegar. Place meat in a glass or enamel dish, pour marinade over and marinate in refrigerator overnight. Dry leg with paper towelling.

Heat butter and oil in potjie and brown meat on all sides. Add onion and sauté until transparent. Heat stock, wine and salt and pour over meat. Sprinkle raisins over. Heat remaining marinade and add. Cover and simmer for $1^1/_2$–2 hours or until meat is nearly tender. Add remaining vegetables, replace lid and simmer for a further 30 minutes. Add more meat stock during cooking process if necessary.
Serves 6

Leg of lamb in the potjie

Lamb knuckles with rice
Potjie No. 3

This potjiekos recipe comprises ordinary, everyday ingredients, and will not cost a fortune to prepare. It won first prize at a potjiekos competition in 1986 and was so popular that nobody, not even the person with a bird's appetite, could refuse the invitation of a second helping. Be warned, therefore, that when calculating the amount of food per guest, you will need generous portions.

4 lamb shanks, sawn into
   slices (leg and shoulder)
15 ml cooking oil
2 large onions, sliced
salt and freshly ground black
   pepper to taste
about 500 ml meat stock
4 large carrots, sliced
4 large potatoes, cubed
500 ml fresh or frozen peas
500 ml uncooked rice

Heat oil in potjie and brown meat a few pieces at a time. Remove and set aside. Add onion and sauté until transparent. Meanwhile season the meat with salt and pepper. Make sure you use enough seasoning to take into account the vegetables and rice, which are added later. Add heated stock, cover with lid and simmer for 45–60 minutes or until meat is almost tender. Add carrots and simmer for another 10 minutes, then add potatoes and simmer for 5 minutes. Finally add peas and rice, ensuring that rice is covered with liquid. Replace lid after each addition. Simmer very slowly for 20 minutes or until rice is cooked. Stir carefully to mix and serve with Potbrood (page 84) and a fresh pineapple salad.
Serves 12

Indonesian lamb potjie
Potjie No. 3

This is a delicious curry. The sour cream makes a rich gravy and the fresh coriander leaves give it a lovely fragrance.

1 kg boned leg of lamb, cubed
1 kg boned shoulder of lamb,
   cubed
15 ml cooking oil
2 large onions, chopped
20 ml garlic and ginger paste
15 ml meat masala
15 ml ground cumin
8 curry leaves
30 ml chutney
3 sticks cinnamon
5 ml turmeric
2 large tomatoes, skinned
   and chopped
75 ml chopped fresh coriander
   leaves
250 ml meat stock
250 ml sour cream
4 potatoes, halved
2 brinjals with peel, cut
   into chunks
30 ml garam masala

Brown meat in heated oil. Add onion and sauté until transparent. Add remaining ingredients, except potatoes, brinjals and garam masala. Cover with lid and simmer slowly for 1^1/$_2$–2 hours. Arrange layers of potato and brinjal on top of meat. Replace lid and simmer for a further 1 hour. Stir in garam masala just before serving.
Serves 6–8

Lamb in a blanket
Potjie Nos. 1 and 3

1 lamb chine or 2 necks of
   lamb, sawn into slices (1 kg)
2 large onions, sliced
1 clove garlic, crushed
2 whole cloves
5 black peppercorns
5 whole allspice
1 bay leaf
5 ml ground coriander
7 ml salt
30 ml wine vinegar
500 ml meat stock

DOUGH BLANKET
250 ml cake flour
5 ml baking powder
1 ml salt
85 g butter
1 egg
85 ml milk

Remove excess fat from meat. Rub inside of potjie with a piece of discarded fat. Add meat a few pieces at a time, and brown. Add onion and garlic and sauté until transparent. Tie cloves, peppercorns, allspice and bay leaf in a muslin bag and add to meat together with coriander and salt. Heat vinegar and stock in a separate, smaller potjie and add to meat. Cover and simmer for 1^1/$_2$–2 hours or until meat is tender. Replenish stock if necessary. Spoon out a little of the liquid and set it aside to serve as gravy as the pastry will absorb most of the liquid.

To make blanket, sift dry ingredients together. Cut butter into small pieces and lightly rub into flour with fingertips. Beat egg and milk together and stir into flour and butter mixture. The mixture should be the consistency of batter. Pour batter on top of meat and spread to cover. Replace lid and simmer for 30 minutes until the dough is cooked.
Serves 6

Potjie tomato bredie

Potjie No. 2 or 3

12 neck slices or thick rib
  lamb chops
15 ml butter
15 ml cooking oil
4 large onions, sliced
2–3 cloves garlic, chopped
6 large ripe tomatoes,
  skinned and chopped
10 ml salt
freshly ground black pepper
  to taste
15 ml brown sugar
2 ml ground cinnamon
6 potatoes, peeled and
  quartered
500 ml meat stock
  (if necessary)

Cut off excess fat. Slash fat edges to prevent curling during cooking. Brown meat in heated butter and oil. Remove and set aside. Add onion and garlic and sauté until transparent. Replace meat on top of onion and garlic and spoon tomato on top. Season with salt and pepper and add sugar and cinnamon to meat. Arrange potatoes on top of tomato and add heated meat stock if necessary. Cover with lid and simmer for 1½–2 hours or until meat and potatoes are tender and tomato has formed a pulp. Serve with rice or Stywepap (page 77).
Serves 6

Boland potjie

Potjie Nos. ½ and 2 and Flat-bottomed
Potjie No. 3

cooking oil to brown meat
8 neck of lamb slices,
  15 mm thick
8 lamb knuckles, 15 mm thick
8 pork knuckles, 15 mm thick
8 small onions
10 ml salt
meat stock
8 carrots, each cut into
  3 pieces
3 large potatoes, cubed
24 young green beans, halved
6 baby marrows, each cut into
  3 pieces
250 g button mushrooms
2 large onions, finely chopped
6 large ripe tomatoes, skinned
  and diced
2–3 cloves garlic, thinly sliced
2–3 drops Tabasco sauce
15 ml soy sauce
15 ml Worcestershire sauce
freshly ground black pepper
  to taste
1 stalk celery, cut into
  5 mm pieces
coarsely chopped fresh parsley

Heat a little oil in the No. 2 potjie, add neck and brown on all sides. Remove and arrange in the centre of a flat-bottomed potjie. Repeat this with the lamb and pork knuckles, placing the lamb in a circle around the neck, then the pork knuckles around the outside edge. Place whole small onions on top and sprinkle with salt. Pour in hot meat stock to almost cover meat. Arrange vegetables on top in layers: carrots, potatoes, then green beans. Cover with lid and allow to simmer. As soon as the potato is almost soft, arrange a layer of baby marrow and then a layer of mushrooms on top. Simmer for about 10 minutes.

Braise onion and tomato in smaller potjie. Add remaining ingredients, except parsley. Simmer for 15 minutes. Spoon over vegetables in flat-bottomed potjie and allow to simmer through. Sprinkle with parsley and serve.
Serves 6

Curried bean potjie

Potjie Nos. 1 and 3

250 ml haricot beans
250 ml kidney beans
1 kg breast of lamb, sawn
  into portions
2 onions, chopped
2 cloves garlic, chopped
3 carrots, sliced
2 stalks celery, cut into pieces
30 ml medium curry powder
5 ml turmeric
5 ml meat masala
1 x 410 g can whole tomatoes,
  chopped
1 bay leaf
7–10 ml salt
freshly ground black pepper
  to taste
500 ml meat stock

Place beans in smaller potjie and cover with cold water. Slowly bring to the boil then boil rapidly for 5 minutes. Remove from heat but keep lid on and allow beans to soak for 1 hour, then drain. Heat larger potjie well without adding oil or butter. Brown meat a few pieces at a time. Add onion, garlic, carrots and celery and sauté until onion is transparent. Add curry powder, turmeric and masala and fry for 2 minutes, stirring well. Arrange beans on top of meat followed by tomatoes, bay leaf, salt, pepper and heated stock. Ensure the beans are well covered. Cover and simmer for 2–3 hours or until beans and meat are tender. Stir carefully to mix.
Serves 6

Lensiekos
(Lamb and lentil potjie)
Potjie Nos. 1 and 3

500 ml brown lentils
1 kg breast of lamb, sawn
　　into portions
2 onions, chopped
2 cloves garlic, chopped
3 carrots, sliced
2 stalks celery, cut into pieces
7–10 ml salt
freshly ground black pepper
　　to taste
1 sprig fresh thyme or
　　5 ml dried
1 sprig fresh rosemary or
　　5 ml dried
1 bay leaf
500 ml meat stock
30 ml vinegar
250 g smoked sausage

Place lentils in smaller potjie, cover with cold water and bring slowly to the boil. Boil for 5 minutes. Remove from heat, but keep lid on and soak for 1 hour. Drain and set aside until required.

Heat larger potjie well and brown meat a few pieces at a time. Add onion, garlic, carrots and celery and sauté until onion is transparent. Heat salt, pepper and herbs with stock and vinegar and add to meat. Add lentils. Make sure the lentils are completely covered with liquid. Add more liquid if necessary. Cover with lid and simmer for 1½–2 hours or until lentils and meat are tender.

Make incisions in sausage and place on top of lentils. Replace lid and simmer for another 15 minutes or until sausage is heated through. Remove sausage, cut into slices and replace. Stir carefully to mix. Serve with a mixed green salad.
Serves 6

Karoo potjie
Potjie No. 3

This traditional Karoo dish, using a simple combination of rice, mutton and potatoes, is a favourite of Peter Veldsman, former cookery editor for *Sarie*. The potatoes become brown and tasty because they absorb the flavoursome meat stock.

30 ml mutton tail fat or 15 ml
　　butter and 15 ml cooking oil
2 large onions, finely chopped
2 cloves garlic, finely chopped
1.5 kg neck of lamb slices
10–15 ml salt
freshly ground black pepper
　　to taste
8 medium potatoes, quartered
　　lengthwise
500 g uncooked rice
2.5 litres meat stock

Heat fat or butter and oil in potjie and sauté onion and garlic until transparent. Remove and set aside. Slash fat edges of meat to prevent curling while cooking. Add meat gradually to potjie and fry until golden brown and crisp. Sprinkle meat with a little salt and pepper. Arrange potatoes on top of meat and sprinkle with remaining salt and pepper. Spread onion and garlic mixture over potatoes. Sprinkle rice over. Heat stock in a separate potjie and pour carefully over rice. Season with more salt and pepper. The liquid should be 25 mm above the rice. Cover with lid and simmer for 1½–2 hours or until the liquid disappears from the top of the rice.
Serves 10

Variations
Add sprigs of fresh herbs, such as thyme, basil and rosemary. Arrange a layer of stoned prunes on top of meat.

Cape pumpkin
bredie in a potjie
Potjie No. 3

500 g lamb shank, sawn
　　into slices
500 g breast of lamb, sawn
　　into portions
2 large onions, sliced
2 cloves garlic, chopped
1 piece root ginger, peeled
　　and chopped
2 whole cloves
1 stick cinnamon
1 chilli, seeded and chopped
4 cardamom pods, crushed
1 bay leaf
1 small piece lemon rind
500 g–1 kg pumpkin, peeled
　　and sliced
knobs of butter
50 ml meat stock or
　　hanepoot wine

Heat potjie until smoking hot, add meat and brown without oil or butter. Remove meat and set aside. Add onion and garlic and sauté in rendered fat until transparent. Arrange meat on top of onion and garlic. Add ginger, cloves, cinnamon, chilli, cardamom, bay leaf and lemon rind. Stir well. Arrange pumpkin on top of meat and dot with butter. Pour heated stock or wine over, cover with lid and simmer very slowly for 1½–2 hours or until meat is tender. Serve with rice.
Serves 6

Variation
Substitute green hubbard squash for pumpkin.

Potjie groenboontjie bredie
Potjie No. 2 or 3

500 g breast of lamb, sawn
    into portions
500 g lamb shank, sawn
    into slices
15 ml butter
15 ml cooking oil
2 large onions, chopped
2 cloves garlic, chopped
500 g green beans, sliced
4 medium potatoes, quartered
500 ml meat stock
10 ml salt
white pepper to taste
grated nutmeg to taste
30 ml lemon juice
50 ml chopped fresh parsley

Brown meat in heated butter and oil. Remove and set aside. Add onion and garlic and sauté until transparent. Arrange meat on top of onion. Place green beans and potatoes on top of meat. Heat meat stock, salt, pepper, nutmeg and lemon juice in a smaller potjie and pour over meat and vegetables. Sprinkle with parsley. Cover with lid and simmer for 1¹/₂–2 hours or until vegetables and meat are tender. Stir carefully to mix ingredients and add a large knob of butter if desired.
Serves 6

Variation
Substitute sheep's tails or beef marrow bones for breast of lamb.

Samp
Potjie No. 3

Most people scorn samp, perhaps because it is not grand enough and rice is usually preferred. Anyone who lives on a farm and harvests their own mealies should seek out a mealie-pounder and try to crush mealies for themselves. Nothing is tastier or healthier.

500 ml samp
2.5 litres water
10 ml salt
250 ml milk
50 g butter

Cover the samp with boiling water and soak overnight or use the quick soaking method used in the Old-fashioned sousboontjies recipe (page 76). Place the drained samp in a potjie and cover with cold water. Cover with lid and bring to the boil. As soon as the samp starts to boil, remove some coals so that it simmers slowly for about 3 hours or until it is soft. Add more boiling water if necessary. If the samp is soft and there is still too much liquid in the pot, remove the lid, place more coals beneath the potjie and allow the liquid to boil off. Add salt and milk to the samp. Allow to simmer slowly for another 30 minutes. Stir in butter and serve with any potjiekos that has its own gravy, or serve as a separate delicacy with plenty of butter and sugar, or sugar and milk.
Serves 8–10

Note: Samp must have a creamy texture and should not be as dry as rice.

Mutton shank potjie
Potjie No. 3

1 kg mutton shank, sawn
    into slices
15 ml cooking oil
250 g onions, sliced
salt and freshly ground black
    pepper to taste
500 ml meat stock
500 g potatoes, sliced
250 g green beans
250 g baby marrows, whole if
    small, otherwise sliced
250 g mushrooms, whole if
    small, sliced if large
4 spring onions
250 g tomatoes, skinned
    and chopped
5 ml chopped fresh oregano
    or 2 ml dried
pinch of ground cloves
1 ml paprika
15 ml fresh rosemary or
    5 ml dried

Brown shank in heated oil. Add onion and sauté until transparent. Season meat with salt and pepper. Pour heated stock over. Arrange vegetables on top of meat in the following order: potatoes, green beans, baby marrows, mushrooms and spring onions. Spoon tomato on top of vegetables. Sprinkle with oregano, cloves, paprika and rosemary. Cover with lid and simmer for 1¹/₂–2 hours or until meat and vegetables are tender. Do not stir during cooking process. Before serving, stir carefully making sure the meat and vegetables do not break up.
Serves 4

Karoo Potjiekos

Pilgrim's potjie
Potjie No. 4

4 sheep's tails (optional)
1.5 kg neck of mutton,
    sawn into slices
1 kg mutton shank,
    sawn into pieces
1 kg mutton breast,
    sawn into portions
2 onions, sliced
1–2 cloves garlic, crushed
1 green pepper, seeded and
    cut into strips
300 g potatoes, peeled
    and sliced
200 g baby carrots
200 g green beans
100 g baby marrows
100 g button mushrooms
½ x 410 g can whole
    tomatoes, chopped
30 ml chopped fresh parsley
5 ml salt
freshly ground black pepper
    to taste
1 bay leaf
50 ml dry white wine
150 ml dry red wine

Place sheep's tails, if using, into potjie, heat slowly and brown. Add remaining meat a few pieces at a time and brown in tail fat. Add onion, garlic and green pepper and sauté until onion and garlic are transparent. Arrange vegetables in layers, in the order listed above, on top of meat. Add tomatoes, parsley, salt and pepper and bay leaf. Pour heated wine over, cover with lid and simmer for 2–3 hours or until meat is tender.
Serves 12

Soutribbetjie with vegetables
Potjie No. 3

1 kg soutribbetjie
1 bay leaf
1–2 whole cloves
1 stick cinnamon
1 piece lemon peel
5 ml dry mustard
8 new potatoes or 4 large
    potatoes
4 large onions, quartered
4 medium carrots, halved
8 baby marrows
4 stalks celery, halved

Tie bay leaf, cloves, cinnamon and lemon peel in a muslin bag. Place meat and spices in potjie, cover with cold water and add mustard. Cover with lid and simmer slowly for 1½ hours or until meat is almost tender.

If using large potatoes, peel and quarter them. Add to potjie together with onions, carrots, baby marrows and celery. Replace lid and simmer for another 30 minutes or until the vegetables are done. Remove meat and arrange on a large meat platter. Arrange vegetables around meat.
Serves 4

Hint
The gravy that remains is delicious with Potbrood (page 84). Break off pieces and dip into gravy. This gravy can also be used as stock or as a soup.

Pumpkin with onions
Flat-bottomed Potjie No. 3

1 kg pumpkin or hubbard
    squash, peeled, seeded
    and sliced
65 ml butter
1 large onion, chopped
50 ml brown sugar
5 ml ground cinnamon
75 ml water

Heat 15 ml butter in flat-bottomed potjie. Add onion and sauté until transparent. Remove onion and set aside. Arrange pumpkin in layers in pot. Sprinkle each layer with a little sugar and cinnamon and dot with remaining butter. Spread sautéed onion over top of pumpkin. Pour heated water over. Cover with lid and place potjie over a small fire for 30–45 minutes or until pumpkin is done. If desired, more sugar and butter may be stirred into the pumpkin, but do not add more water unless absolutely necessary. The pumpkin should be cooked to a golden brown colour without burning or it will be bitter.
Serves 6

From left to right: Soutribbetjie with vegetables, Samp (page 35), Pilgrim's potjie

Pork

Pork and bean potjie
Potjie No. 3 or 4

This recipe is based on traditional French *cassoulet*, a dish of dried beans simmered slowly with a selection of meats.

500 g dried white haricot beans
500 g pork belly (salted or fresh), cut into strips
250 g pork rind, cut into thin strips
2 whole cloves
2 onions, whole
2 cloves garlic, crushed
10 ml salt
freshly ground black pepper to taste
bouquet garni: 4 sprigs parsley, 3 pieces celery, 1 piece
    leek, 2 bay leaves, 1 sprig fresh thyme, all tied together
500 g smoked sausage

Place beans in potjie. Cover with cold water and bring slowly to the boil. Boil for 5 minutes. Remove from heat and allow to stand, covered, for 1 hour. Add pork belly and rind. Stick cloves in onions and add to potjie together with garlic, salt, pepper and bouquet garni. Cover with lid and simmer slowly until meat is tender. Replenish with heated stock if necessary. Make shallow incisions in the sausage and add to potjie 15 minutes before serving. Remove bouquet garni. Slice sausage thickly and return to potjie. Stir gently, then serve with French bread and mixed green salad.
Serves 6

Pork and bean potjie

Pork with sweet potatoes and apple
Flat-bottomed Potjie No. 3

1 kg pork thick rib chops
15 ml butter
15 ml cooking oil
1 onion, chopped
500 g sweet potatoes, peeled
  and sliced
2 green apples, cored, peeled,
  and sliced
15 ml honey or brown sugar
  (optional)
2 whole cloves
2 sticks cinnamon
1 piece lemon peel
250 ml dry white wine
250 ml meat stock
30–50 ml lemon juice
7 ml salt
pepper to taste

Remove rind and excess fat from chops and cut meat into smaller pieces. Heat butter and oil in potjie. Add meat a few pieces at a time and brown. Pour off excess oil. Add onion and sauté gently until transparent. Remove meat and onion and set aside. Arrange half the sweet potatoes in bottom of potjie, follow with half the meat and onion and half the apple. Repeat with remaining sweet potato, meat, onion and apple. Heat remaining ingredients in a smaller potjie and pour over meat. Cover with lid and simmer very slowly for 1^1/$_2$–2 hours or until meat is tender. Remove whole spices.
Serves 6

Pork and ham potjie
Potjie Nos. 1 and 3

1 kg pork breast, sawn
  into portions
500 g ham, cubed
4 onions, chopped
250 g rindless bacon,
  chopped
4 carrots, diced
3 apples, diced
5–7 ml salt
freshly ground black pepper
  to taste
250 ml uncooked rice
250 ml meat stock
250 ml semi-sweet wine
  (stein)
125 ml dry sherry
5 ml prepared mustard

Heat potjie, add pork and ham a few pieces at a time and brown. Add onion and bacon and sauté until onion is transparent. Add carrots and apples and season with salt and pepper. Spoon rice on top of meat and vegetables. Heat stock, wine, sherry and mustard in smaller potjie and add to meat. Cover with lid and simmer slowly for 2–3 hours or until meat is tender.
Serves 6

Pork and brinjal potjie
Potjie No. 3

1.5 kg boneless pork thick rib,
  cubed or 1.5 kg shanks,
  sawn into slices
15 ml cooking oil
4 onions, sliced
8 potatoes, quartered
12 medium carrots
500 g mushrooms
salt and freshly ground black
  pepper to taste
2 large brinjals, cubed
1 x 410 g can mushroom or
  vegetable soup

Heat oil in potjie and brown meat. Add onion, potatoes, carrots and mushrooms in that order, seasoning with salt and pepper between layers. Cover with lid and simmer slowly for 1^1/$_2$ hours or until just cooked. Arrange brinjal on top and pour soup over. Replace lid and simmer for a further 30 minutes or until brinjal is cooked.
Serves 6

Flemish hutspot

Potjie No. 4

This is the recipe with which Thérèse and Jacques Vankeirsbilck won the Kellerprinz potjiekos championship in 1985. It is based on a traditional Flemish hutspot recipe. Hutspot is the Flemish version of the English stew, French ragout or Italian stufato.

15 ml butter or lard
7 onions, chopped
6 cloves garlic, crushed
2 green peppers, seeded and
   cut into quarters
250 g rindless bacon,
   chopped
2 packets pork sausages,
   pricked
1 kg Eisbein
250 ml semi-sweet wine
   (stein)
7 leeks, sliced
1 small bunch celery, cut up
10 large carrots, sliced into
   rings
14 medium potatoes, peeled
1 small bunch curly kale, cut
   into pieces
1 small cabbage, shredded

Heat butter or fat in potjie and add onion, garlic, green pepper and bacon and sauté until vegetables are transparent. Add sausages and Eisbein. Heat wine in separate potjie and pour over meat. Cover with lid and simmer for 20 minutes. Layer remaining ingredients in order listed, replace lid and simmer slowly for 2–2$^1/_2$ hours. Do not remove lid to peep. When cooked, stir carefully without breaking up sausages. Serve with Wine bread (page 85) and Herbed mustard sauce (page 78).
Serves 10

Pork potjie with ginger sauce

Potjie Nos. 1 and 3

15 ml butter
15 ml cooking oil
1 kg boneless pork thick rib,
   cubed
1 onion, chopped
2 stalks leafy celery, sliced
6 pickling onions
6 baby carrots or 3 large
250 ml meat stock
30–45 ml vinegar
5 ml salt
freshly ground black pepper
   to taste
1 bay leaf
1 sprig fresh thyme or
   2 ml dried
2 gingersnaps

Heat butter and oil in larger potjie, add meat a few pieces at a time and brown. Add onion, celery, pickling onions and carrots and fry lightly until onion is transparent. Heat stock, vinegar, salt, pepper, bay leaf and thyme in smaller potjie. Pour over meat. Cover with lid and simmer for 1$^1/_2$–2 hours or until meat is tender. Place gingersnaps on top of meat, pressing them into the juice, and simmer for another 10 minutes until they become floury. Stir gently to mix ingredients. Serve with Stampkoring (page 79) or Samp (page 35).
Serves 8

Spiced pork and rice potjie

Potjie No. 3

500 g boneless lean thick rib
   of pork, cubed
15 ml cooking oil
1 medium onion, chopped
1 clove garlic, chopped
15 ml chopped root ginger
30 ml mild curry powder
1 whole clove
1 bay leaf
4 cardamom pods
5 ml crushed coriander seeds
1 stick cinnamon
250 ml uncooked rice
1 x 410 g can pineapple rings
400 ml meat stock
30 ml wine vinegar
5–7 ml salt

Heat cooking oil, add meat and brown. Add onion, garlic and ginger and sauté until onion is transparent. Add curry powder and remaining spices and fry for about 2 minutes. Remove meat or use a clean potjie. Place half the rice into bottom of potjie and arrange half the meat on top. Add another layer of rice and meat. Drain pineapple, reserving juice. Arrange pineapple rings on top of meat. Heat pineapple juice, stock, vinegar and salt in smaller potjie and pour over meat and rice. Cover with lid and simmer for 1$^1/_2$–2 hours or until meat is cooked and liquid has been absorbed by rice. Serve with braaied bananas and chutney.
Serves 4

Pork curry

Potjie No. 2 or 3

1 kg boneless pork, cubed
   (thick rib or leg)
15 ml cooking oil
1 onion, chopped
1 clove garlic, crushed
15 ml mild curry powder
200 ml hanepoot
200 ml meat stock
30 ml wine vinegar
5 ml turmeric
30 ml chopped root ginger
1 bay leaf
1 stick cinnamon
5 cardamom pods
10 ml salt
freshly ground black pepper
   to taste
50 ml desiccated coconut
50 ml seedless raisins
2 green apples, cored, peeled
   and cut into wedges
1 carrot, grated

Heat oil in potjie, add meat a few pieces at a time and brown. Add onion and garlic and sauté until transparent. Add curry powder and fry for about 2 minutes. Heat wine, stock, vinegar, turmeric, ginger, bay leaf, cinnamon, cardamom, salt and pepper in a smaller potjie. Pour over meat. Arrange remaining ingredients on top of meat. Cover with lid and simmer for $1^{1}/_{2}$–2 hours or until meat is tender. Stir very carefully, then serve with yellow rice and raisins and chutney.
Serves 8

Pork with beer and mustard bread

Potjie No. 2 or 3

4 rashers rindless bacon,
   cut into pieces
1 kg boneless thick rib of pork,
   cubed
2 medium onions, chopped
2 large carrots, sliced
2 stalks celery, chopped
350 ml beer
125 ml meat stock
1 bay leaf
5 ml salt
freshly ground black pepper
   to taste
5 ml grated lemon rind
15 ml lemon juice
250 ml fresh or frozen peas

MUSTARD BREAD

4 slices bread (white,
   whole-wheat or French)
60 g soft butter
15 ml prepared French mustard

Fry bacon in potjie until crisp. Remove and set aside. Add meat a few pieces at a time and brown. Add onion and sauté until transparent. Add carrots and celery and sauté lightly. Heat beer, stock, bay leaf and seasoning in a smaller potjie and add to meat. Cover with lid and simmer for $1^{1}/_{2}$–2 hours or until meat is tender. Season with lemon rind and juice. Add peas and simmer a further 5 minutes. Meanwhile, blend butter and mustard together and spread on bread. (Cut large slices in half but leave French bread slices whole.) Place butter-side up on top of meat. Replace lid and simmer for another 10 minutes until the pan juices have soaked into the bread. Do not stir. Serve with a crisp green salad.
Serves 6

Quince and pork potjie

Potjie Nos. 1 and 3

15 ml cooking oil
15 ml butter
2 large onions, chopped
2 cloves garlic, chopped
2 pork shanks (about 1 kg)
3 quinces
250 ml meat stock
250 ml dry white wine
15 ml wine vinegar
   or lemon juice
2 whole cloves
pinch of grated nutmeg
5 ml ground coriander
15 ml brown sugar, golden
   syrup or honey (optional)
5–7 ml salt
freshly ground black pepper
   to taste

Heat butter and oil in larger potjie. Add onion and garlic and sauté lightly until transparent. Remove and set aside. Arrange a layer of meat on bottom of pot and follow with half the onion and garlic mixture. Wash quinces and rub fine hairs off with a rough cloth, then core and cut into wedges. Arrange half the quince on top of meat. Repeat layers of meat, onion and quince. Heat remaining ingredients in smaller potjie and pour over meat and quince in larger pot. Cover with lid and simmer slowly for 2–$2^{1}/_{2}$ hours or until meat is tender. Add more stock if necessary.
Serves 6

Variation
Canned fruit may be substituted, but omit the sugar, syrup or honey mentioned in the ingredients above. If using canned quince, taste gravy in pot and add 15 ml lemon juice if too sweet.

Pork ribs with braai sauce

Potjie No. 3

1.5 kg pork breast, sawn
   into portions
10 baby potatoes
250 g baby green beans

BRAAI SAUCE

2 large onions, chopped
2 cloves garlic, crushed
15 ml cooking oil
250 ml meat stock
125 ml brown vinegar
250 ml tomato sauce
30 ml Worcestershire sauce
5 ml brown sugar
5 ml salt
freshly ground black pepper
   to taste
1 ml ground cloves
1 ml ground ginger
30 ml chutney
30 ml sweet sherry

First make the braai sauce: Mix all the ingredients, except sherry, in a small potjie and simmer for 30–45 minutes until flavours are thoroughly blended. Add sherry during last 5 minutes of cooking time, then set sauce aside.

Heat larger potjie, place meat into potjie, fat-side down, and brown. Add braai sauce and simmer for 1¹/₂–2 hours or until meat is almost cooked. Scrub potatoes and place on top of meat. Add green beans. Cover with lid and simmer for a further 30 minutes until potatoes are cooked.
Serves 10

Pork potjie with herbed dumplings

Potjie No. 6

3–4 pork shanks, cleaned and
   sawn into pieces
50–75 ml cooking oil
7 ml salt
3 ml pepper
3–4 cloves garlic
3 pieces root ginger or
   5 ml powdered ginger
250 ml dry white wine
250 ml meat stock
vegetables in season (whole
   small potatoes, baby
   carrots, baby marrows,
   cauliflower, beans, etc.)
whole pickling onions

HERBED DUMPLINGS

500 ml cake flour
10 ml baking powder
2 ml salt
2 ml onion salt
5 ml dried parsley
250 ml milk
1 egg

Heat oil in potjie, add meat and turn to seal. Heat remaining ingredients, except vegetables, in a smaller potjie and pour over meat. Simmer over medium heat for about 2 hours.

Prepare dumplings 30 minutes prior to serving: Sift all dry ingredients together. Beat milk and egg together. Add to dry ingredients and mix well. Allow to stand for about 20 minutes before cooking.

Add vegetables to potjie and simmer for a further 20 minutes. Add dumplings by the spoonful, replace lid and simmer for a further 10–12 minutes. Do not remove lid until cooking is complete.
Serves 6

Note: If extra liquid is needed, add stock or wine rather than water.

SPEK AND BACON

There is often confusion over these two ingredients and more than one recipe has failed because the incorrect ingredient has landed in the potjie. Spek is pork fat from the belly of a baconer and is usually cut in slabs. Spek also refers to the fat from cured or smoked pork and is particularly popular in Germany and other European countries where it is used either as the basic fat for browning meat in the preparation of venison or to lard lean beef cuts. In traditional South African cooking, spek plays an important part: it is used in the making of boerewors, for larding lean beef cuts, in the preparation of venison and, of course, to 'break in' a new potjie or any other cast-iron cooking utensil, such as a frying pan. Bacon, on the other hand, comprises layers of meat and fat, which have been pickled and/or smoked. Unsmoked bacon is known as 'green bacon'.

A Taste of Namibia

Creamy potato and pork potjie

Potjie No. 3

250 g rindless bacon,
    coarsely chopped
 6 spring onions, chopped
    or 1 large onion, chopped
4 cloves garlic, crushed
500 g pork belly, sliced
500 g pork short ribs,
    sawn into portions
1 kg potatoes, peeled and sliced
10 ml salt
freshly ground black pepper
    to taste
250 ml meat or chicken stock
250 ml thin cream
1 sprig fresh thyme or
    5 ml dried
1 piece celery stalk
1 bay leaf

Fry bacon until crisp. Add onion and garlic and sauté until transparent. Remove onion mixture from potjie and set aside. Add meat a few pieces at a time and brown. Remove meat and set aside. Arrange ingredients in potjie in the following layers: half the potato, then half the bacon and onion mixture and finally the pork belly. Repeat these layers, ending with a layer of ribs. Sprinkle each layer with a little salt and pepper, stock and cream. Tie the thyme, celery and bay leaf together to make bouquet garni and place on top. (If using dried thyme, sprinkle on top.) Cover with lid and simmer slowly for 1½–2 hours or until meat and potatoes are tender. Remove bouquet garni.
Serves 6–8

Kasseler rib with red cabbage

Potjie No.3

6 Kasseler chops
15 ml butter
15 ml cooking oil
1 onion, cut into rings
½ red cabbage, shredded
2 green apples, cored
    and cut into rings
2 whole cloves
5 ml salt
pepper to taste
250 ml dry red wine
30 ml vinegar
15 ml brown sugar or
    15 ml apple jelly

Heat butter and oil in potjie and lightly brown meat. Remove meat from potjie and set aside. Sauté onion lightly until transparent. Remove from potjie. Arrange meat on bottom of potjie, place cabbage and onion on top of meat followed by apple rings. Heat remaining ingredients and pour over meat. Cover with lid and simmer slowly for 1½ hours or until meat is tender. Serve with vetkoek.
Serves 6

Liver rolls on a skewer

250 g stoned prunes
250 ml sweet red muscadel
500 g sheep's liver
30 ml lemon juice
15 ml chopped fresh thyme
    or 5 ml dried
250 g rindless bacon
15 ml mild prepared mustard

Soak prunes in muscadel for 1 hour. Clean liver by removing outer membrane. Cut liver into large cubes, sprinkle lemon juice and thyme over and marinate for 1 hour. Cut bacon rashers in half and stretch each with the back of a knife. Spread mustard over bacon. Roll a piece of bacon around each cube of liver and prune. Thread liver and prunes alternately onto wooden skewers. Grill over coals until done and serve immediately. Serve as a starter.
Serves 6

Quick beer bread

Potjie No. 3

550 ml white bread flour
600 ml cracked wheat
5 ml salt
1 packet instant yeast
5 ml caraway seeds (optional)
350 ml beer
30 ml honey
15 ml melted butter
100 ml warm water

*From left to right: Liver
rolls on a skewer, Quick
beer bread, Kasseler rib
with red cabbage,
Creamy potato
and pork potjie*

Mix flour, cracked wheat, salt, yeast and caraway seeds (if using) in a large bowl. Heat the beer slightly. Mix with honey, melted butter and warm water and add to flour mixture. Stir until dough becomes easily manageable. Turn out onto floured surface and knead for about 4 minutes or until the dough is smooth and comes away from the surface easily. Form dough into a ball, flatten the top slightly and place in buttered potjie. Brush dough and inside of lid with melted butter. Place lid on pot and place in a warm draughtless position for about 45 minutes until the dough has doubled in size. Place pot on slow fire with a few small coals on top of lid and bake for 45–60 minutes or until the bread sounds hollow when tapped. Turn out while still hot and serve immediately with butter.

Game

Sweet-and-sour venison
Potjie Nos. 1 and 3

125 g spek, diced
15 ml cooking oil
15 ml butter
2 onions, chopped
2 cloves garlic, chopped
1 kg boneless venison (leg or thick rib), cubed
5 ml salt
freshly ground black pepper to taste
250 ml meat stock
200 ml pineapple juice
30–45 ml wine vinegar
1 bay leaf
15 ml soy sauce
1 x 410 g can pineapple pieces
125 g stoned prunes
8 pickling onions, peeled

Fry spek in larger potjie until crisp. Add oil and butter to fat in potjie and heat thoroughly. Add onion and garlic and sauté until transparent. Remove onion and spek mixture and set aside. Brown meat in remaining fat. Spoon onion and spek mixture on top of meat. Season meat with salt and pepper. Heat stock, pineapple juice, vinegar, bay leaf and soy sauce in smaller potjie and pour over meat. Cover with lid and simmer slowly for 3–4 hours or until meat is almost tender. Replenish with heated stock if necessary. Arrange pineapple pieces, prunes and pickling onions on top of meat. Replace lid and simmer for a further 30 minutes. Remove bay leaf and serve venison with Stampkoring in the potjie (page 79). *Serves 6*

Sweet-and-sour venison, served with Spiced peaches (page 80) and Potbrood (page 84)

Creamy rabbit potjie

Potjie Nos. 1 and 3

1 x 1.5 kg rabbit
250 g smoked bacon
2 onions, chopped
1 stalk celery, chopped
1 small carrot, chopped
500 g brown mushrooms,
    sliced
30 ml cake flour
250 ml chicken or venison
    stock
250 ml dry white wine
3 small sprigs fresh thyme
    or 5 ml dried
3 bay leaves
5 ml salt
freshly ground black pepper
    to taste
2 slices white bread
15 ml prepared mustard
30 ml brandy or whisky
    (optional)
125 ml sour cream

Cut rabbit into portions and dice bacon. Fry bacon in potjie until crisp. Remove and set aside. Add a little extra butter or cooking oil to fat in potjie if necessary. Add onion, celery, carrot and mushrooms and sauté until onion is transparent. Remove vegetables and set aside. Brown meat in left-over fat and then sprinkle with flour. Heat stock, wine, herbs and seasoning in smaller potjie, then pour over meat. Arrange bacon and vegetables in layers on top of meat. Cover with lid and simmer slowly over a very small fire for 1½–2 hours or until meat is tender.

Spread bread with mustard and cut slices in half. Place mustard-side down on top of meat. Replace lid and simmer for another 30 minutes or until meat is completely tender.

Using a small container (an enamel coffee mug will do) heat brandy or whisky very carefully over fire. Set alight and pour flaming brandy over meat. Pour cream over meat and allow to simmer for a further 2 minutes. Remove thyme sprigs and bay leaves and serve meat with Potjie roast potatoes (page 77) or Potbrood (page 84).
Serves 6

Hunter's pot

Potjie Nos. 1 and 3

125 g rindless bacon, chopped
1 onion, chopped
1 clove garlic, chopped
350 g brown mushrooms,
    sliced
15 ml butter
15 ml cooking oil
6 kudu Scotch fillet steaks
125 ml dry red wine
250 ml meat stock
15 ml tomato paste
15 ml lemon juice
5 ml salt
freshly ground black pepper
    to taste
15 ml chopped fresh parsley

Fry bacon in larger potjie until crisp. Add onion, garlic and mushrooms to rendered fat and sauté until transparent. Remove bacon and vegetables and set aside. Place butter and oil in potjie and heat. Add meat and brown a few pieces at a time. Place meat at bottom of potjie and arrange vegetables on top. Heat wine, stock, tomato paste, lemon juice, salt and pepper together in smaller potjie and add to meat. Cover with lid and simmer for 2–3 hours or until meat is tender. Sprinkle with parsley and serve.
Serves 6

From back to front:
Creamy rabbit potjie, Hunter's pot

Jugged venison
Potjie No. 3

2 onions, chopped
1 clove garlic, finely chopped
15 ml butter
2 kg venison with bones
3 sheep's tails or 1 neck of
   mutton, sliced
1 pork rind with a thick layer
   of fat
5 whole cloves
5 ml ground coriander
5 black peppercorns
2 bay leaves
4 whole allspice
1 sprig parsley
30 ml wine vinegar
500 ml meat or venison stock
15 ml smooth apricot jam,
   maroela or apple jelly

Heat butter in potjie and sauté onions and garlic until transparent. Place meat, tails or neck and pork rind on top of onions. Heat cloves, coriander, peppercorns, bay leaves, allspice, parsley, vinegar and stock and add to meat. Cover with lid and simmer slowly for 2–2^1/$_2$ hours or until meat is tender. Remove meat from bones. Replace meat and remove bay leaves and whole spices. Stir in jam or jelly.
Serves 6

Variation
If desired, spoon dumplings on top of meat 15 minutes before end of cooking time.

DUMPLINGS
250 ml cake flour
10 ml baking powder
2 ml salt
15 ml butter
1 egg, beaten
125 ml milk, or milk and water

Sift dry ingredients. Rub in butter. Beat egg and milk together and add to flour mixture. Mix with a wooden spoon to a soft consistency. Add an extra 250 ml heated stock to meat in pot and spoon dumplings on top of meat. Cover and simmer for 15 minutes or until dumplings are feather-light and cooked. Do not peep into potjie during cooking process.

Another method is to half fill a No. 1 or 2 potjie with water or stock. Bring to the boil, spoon in dumplings and simmer for 10–15 minutes or until dumplings are light and cooked. Serve dumplings with meat.

Ostrich fillet with quince
Potjie Nos. 1 and 3

1 kg ostrich fillet, cubed
15 ml cooking oil
15 ml butter
6 pickling onions, cleaned
250 ml dry white wine
250 ml meat stock
5 ml salt
freshly ground black pepper
   to taste
2 large quinces
100 ml seedless raisins
5–15 ml sugar
4 potatoes, peeled and cubed

Brown meat in heated butter and oil in larger potjie. Add onions and sauté until glossy. Heat wine and stock in smaller potjie and add to meat. Season meat with salt and pepper, cover with lid and simmer for about 1 hour. Meanwhile, rub quinces to remove hairs and cut into wedges, pips and all. Place on top of meat with remaining ingredients and replace lid. Simmer for 20 minutes.
Serves 6

Guinea-fowl with lentils
Potjie Nos. 1 and 3

1 guinea-fowl
250 g spek
30 ml butter
2 medium carrots, diced
2 onions, sliced
2 whole cloves
6 black peppercorns
1 bay leaf
1 sprig fresh thyme or
   5 ml dried
7 ml salt
freshly ground black pepper
   to taste
250 ml dry white wine
250 ml meat stock
500 g brown lentils, soaked
   overnight in cold water

Wash guinea-fowl thoroughly under cold running water. Cut into portions. Dice spek and keep pork rind to cook with guinea-fowl. Place spek and rind in potjie and fry until crisp. Remove spek and set aside. Add butter to fat in potjie. Add carrot and onion and sauté until transparent. Remove from potjie and set aside. Add guinea-fowl a few pieces at a time and brown. Spoon vegetables on top of guinea-fowl and sprinkle with spek. Tie spices in a muslin bag and heat with remaining ingredients, except lentils, in smaller potjie. Add to guinea-fowl. Cover with lid and simmer for 3–4 hours or until guinea-fowl is tender. Drain lentils and place on top of guinea-fowl. Replace lid and simmer for another 30–40 minutes or until lentils are tender, adding more warm stock if necessary.
Serves 6

Variation
Add 2 peeled green apples with the lentils.

Ostrich fillet with green peppercorns
Potjie No. 2

2.5 kg ostrich fillet
250 ml seasoned cake flour
50 ml cooking oil
40 g butter
125 ml chopped spring onions
15 ml chopped fresh rosemary
250 g brown mushrooms,
    sliced
15 ml green peppercorns
50 ml chopped fresh parsley
75 ml brandy
50 ml dry sherry
375 ml rosé wine
15 pickling onions, peeled
10 small carrots
8 small potatoes
250 g frozen or cooked
    chopped spinach
125 ml cream or sour cream
15 ml cake flour
salt to taste

Cut the ostrich fillet into 25 mm cubes and roll in seasoned flour. Heat half the butter and oil in the potjie. Add spring onions and rosemary, and fry lightly until onion is transparent. Add mushrooms, peppercorns and parsley and sauté for 3–5 minutes. Remove from heat and set aside. Reheat potjie, add remaining butter and oil and brown meat a few pieces at a time. Heat brandy in a small container, pour over meat and set alight. Lift potjie further off the fire and add heated sherry and wine. Simmer, uncovered, until the liquid is reduced by half. This will take about 30 minutes. Now place the vegetables in circles on top of the meat, starting with the onions on the outside, then the carrots and the potatoes in the middle. Cover with lid and simmer for about 1 hour or until meat is tender.

Blend the spinach (thawed if frozen), cream and flour thoroughly. Pour carefully over food in the potjie and replace lid for another 15 minutes. Season with a little salt if necessary. Serve with rice and a salad or with Spätzle (page 78).
Serves 6

Sweet-and-sour venison shoulder
Potjie Nos. 1 and 3

1.5 kg shoulder of venison,
    boned
15 ml French mustard
6 rashers rindless bacon
1 onion, chopped
15 ml butter
15 ml cooking oil
5 ml salt
freshly ground black pepper
    to taste
125 g dried apricots
125 g stoned prunes

MARINADE
1 clove garlic, crushed
1 bay leaf
4 juniper berries
4 black peppercorns
30 ml wine vinegar
5 ml brown sugar
1 stick cinnamon
2 whole cloves
1 ml salt
250 ml rooibos tea
250 ml meat stock
50 ml cooking oil

Spread the inside of the meat with mustard. Arrange bacon rashers on top of mustard. Sauté onion in heated butter and oil in smaller potjie. Allow to cool slightly and then spoon over bacon. Roll meat up and tie with string. Mix marinade ingredients together and pour over meat. Allow meat to marinate in refrigerator overnight. Remove meat from marinade and dry thoroughly with paper towelling. Reserve marinade. Heat another 15 ml each of butter and oil in larger potjie and brown meat on all sides. Season meat with salt and pepper. Heat marinade in smaller potjie and add to meat. Cover with lid and simmer slowly for 2–3 hours or until meat is tender. Arrange dried fruit on top of meat and simmer for a further 30 minutes.
Serves 6

Note: Marinades are not always necessary in potjiekos unless of course you have a specific flavour in mind and even then, the marinade should never be overpowering because the subtle, distinctive venison flavour would be lost. It is not always necessary to marinate game overnight and in fact, smaller cuts need only a few hours.

Hunter's Potjie

Venison soup

Potjie Nos. 2 and 3

1 venison shank
 or about 500 g bones
1 carrot
1 onion, stuck with
 2 whole cloves
1 sprig fresh parsley
1 sprig fresh thyme
5 black peppercorns
1 bay leaf
5 juniper berries
5 ml salt
15 ml vinegar
4 rashers bacon,
 rind removed and chopped
2 onions, chopped
1 clove garlic, chopped
1 stalk celery, chopped
250 ml brown lentils
30 ml chopped fresh parsley

First prepare stock by placing meat, carrot, onion, parsley, thyme, peppercorns, bay leaf, juniper berries, salt and vinegar into the smaller potjie. Cover with cold water and bring to the boil. Lower heat by removing coals and simmer for 2–3 hours, skimming off foam. Strain stock through a sieve. Cut meat off bones and set aside. Discard bones. Fry bacon until crisp in larger potjie. Add onion, garlic and celery and sauté until transparent. Add lentils and stock. Cover with lid and simmer for 45 minutes or until lentils are tender. Return meat to potjie, adjust seasoning, sprinkle with chopped parsley and serve.
Serves 6

Kudu liver rosé

Potjie No. 3

1.2 kg kudu liver
250 g streaky bacon,
 rind removed
30 g butter
15 ml fresh basil
 or 5 ml dried
250 ml chicken stock
500 g mixed vegetables
 (green beans, baby
 marrow, pickling onions,
 broccoli, etc.)
125 ml rosé wine
50 ml fruit chutney
250 ml sour cream
15 ml cornflour
7–10 ml salt
freshly ground black pepper
 to taste

MARINADE

30 ml cooking oil
50 ml rosé wine
2 ml salt
2 ml paprika
1 bay leaf
1 onion, chopped
1 large clove garlic, chopped

First make the marinade: Mix all the ingredients together. Place liver in marinade and marinate for 1 hour.

Remove liver from marinade and pat dry. Reserve marinade. Make small incisions in liver and stuff with bacon strips. (If necessary, tie liver up with string.) Heat butter in potjie, add liver and brown quickly. Add marinade and basil. Cover and simmer for 45 minutes or until liver is almost tender. Add warmed stock and vegetables and simmer until vegetables are tender. Remove liver and vegetables and keep warm.

Add wine, chutney and sour cream to pan juices. Thicken liquid with a cornflour and water paste if necessary. Remove bay leaf, season with salt and pepper and pour gravy over liver and vegetables.
Serves 6

Guinea-fowl in red wine

Potjie Nos. 1 and 3

125 g spek, diced
15 ml butter
15 ml cooking oil
2 onions, chopped
2 cloves garlic, chopped
1 guinea-fowl, cut into portions
1 small carrot, chopped
1 stalk celery, chopped
1 bay leaf
2 sprigs fresh thyme
15 ml chopped fresh oregano
 or 5 ml dried
5–7 ml salt
freshly ground black pepper
 to taste
200 ml dry red wine
100 ml meat stock
350 ml brown mushrooms
30 ml chopped fresh parsley

Fry spek in larger potjie until crisp. Remove and set aside. Add butter and oil to remaining fat and sauté onion and garlic until transparent. Remove and set aside. Add guinea-fowl portions and brown on all sides. Spoon onion mixture, carrot, celery and spek on top. Add herbs, salt and pepper. Heat wine and stock together in smaller potjie and pour over guinea-fowl. Cover and simmer slowly for 2–3 hours or until tender. Arrange mushrooms on top and sprinkle with parsley. Replace lid and simmer for a further 15 minutes or until mushrooms are tender.
Serves 6

Venison shin in the pot

Venison shin in the pot

Potjie No. 3

4 rashers rindless bacon

1.5 kg venison shank, sawn into slices

1 onion, chopped

2 cloves garlic, chopped

1 bay leaf

3 black peppercorns

4 juniper berries (optional)

350 ml venison stock

30 ml wine vinegar

15 ml smooth apricot jam

125 g dried apricots

125 g prunes

6 small carrots

1 stalk celery, cut into chunks

Fry bacon in potjie until crisp. Remove and set aside. Brown meat in rendered fat, adding more butter and oil if necessary. Add onion and garlic and sauté until transparent. Add bay leaf, peppercorns and juniper berries to stock, together with vinegar and apricot jam, and heat. Pour over meat. Cover with lid and simmer slowly for 2–3 hours or until meat is tender. Replenish stock if necessary. Remove bones and scrape meat off bones. Remove bay leaf and whole spices. Replace meat and arrange fruit and vegetables on top. Cover with lid and simmer for a further 30 minutes.

Serves 6

Poultry

Duck and pineapple potjie
Potjie Nos. 1 and 3

1 duck, cut into portions
15 ml cooking oil
1 onion, chopped
2 cloves garlic, chopped
1 carrot, cut into strips
1 green pepper, seeded and cut into strips
2 stalks celery, thinly sliced on the diagonal
5–7 ml salt
freshly ground black pepper to taste
30 ml chopped root ginger or 10 ml ground ginger
30 ml cake flour
1 x 439 g canned pineapple pieces,
    drained or 1 pineapple, peeled and cubed
15 ml soy sauce
250 ml chicken stock
30–45 ml wine vinegar
5 ml brown sugar
10 spring onions, cleaned and left whole

Heat oil in potjie, add duck and brown a few pieces at a time. Remove and set aside. Add onion, garlic, carrot, green pepper and celery. Sauté until onion is transparent. Remove vegetables and set aside. Pour off excess oil. Replace duck. Add salt, pepper, ginger and flour and stir to avoid burning. Place sautéed vegetables and then pineapple on top of duck. Heat soy sauce, chicken stock, vinegar and sugar in separate small potjie and pour over duck. Cover with lid and simmer slowly for 1–1$^1/_2$ hours or until duck is tender. Place spring onions on top of duck and vegetables, replace lid and simmer for a further 20 minutes until the spring onions are heated through. Stir potjie carefully and serve.
Serves 4

Duck and pineapple potjie

Spiced chicken with yoghurt

Potjie Nos. 2 or 3

1 chicken, cut into portions
1 piece chilli, seeded
2 bay leaves
5 ml turmeric
2 ml ground cloves
5 ml cardamom pods
2 ml cumin seeds
5 ml ground coriander
2 ml grated nutmeg
1 stick cinnamon
2 cloves garlic, chopped
5 ml ground ginger
   or 15 ml chopped root ginger
15 ml lemon juice
500 ml natural yoghurt
2 onions, finely chopped
7–10 ml salt
pepper to taste
15 ml cornflour (optional)

Place chilli, bay leaves and all spices in a pestle and mortar and grind into a paste with garlic and ginger. Mix lemon juice with yoghurt and add to spice mixture. Add onion. Place chicken in glass or ceramic dish and pour yoghurt mixture over. Allow to marinate in refrigerator overnight, turning occasionally.

   Place chicken in potjie and heat slowly to prevent mixture burning. Simmer for 1–1¹/₂ hours or until chicken is tender. Sprinkle with salt and pepper. If necessary, thicken liquid by mixing cornflour with a little cold water to form a paste. Add to the potjie and simmer for a few minutes. Alternatively, set potjie on high heat for a few minutes to reduce liquid. Serve with Roosterkoek (page 83) and Tomato sambal (page 79).
Serves 6

Chicken breasts with creamy mushrooms

Potjie No. 2 or 3

8 chicken breasts (approx. 1 kg)
15 ml butter
15 ml cooking oil
1 onion, chopped
250 g mushrooms, sliced
15 ml chopped fresh parsley
   or 5 ml dried
15 ml chopped fresh mixed
   herbs or 5 ml dried
5 ml prepared mustard
5–7 ml salt
pepper to taste
2 x 170 g cans evaporated
   milk
8 small or 4 large potatoes,
   quartered
15 ml cake flour (if necessary)

Heat butter and oil in potjie, add chicken gradually and brown. Add onion and mushrooms and fry lightly for a few minutes until onion is transparent. Mix parsley, herbs, mustard, salt and pepper and spread over chicken. Pour milk over chicken. Arrange potatoes on top, cover with lid and simmer for 1–1¹/₂ hours or until chicken is tender. Thicken with flour, if necessary. Serve with rice or Stampkoring (page 79).
Serves 6

Chicken with creamy asparagus sauce

Potjie Nos. 1 and 2

10 chicken thighs
15 ml butter
15 ml cooking oil
10 pickling onions, peeled
10 baby potatoes
1 x 410 g can cream of
   asparagus soup
50 ml sherry
125 ml chicken stock

Heat butter and oil in potjie and brown chicken on all sides. Add onions and fry until golden brown. Arrange potatoes on top of chicken. Heat soup, sherry and stock in smaller potjie and pour over chicken. Cover with lid and simmer slowly for 1–1¹/₂ hours or until chicken is tender.
Serves 6

Easy chicken pot

Potjie Nos. 1 and 3

1 medium whole chicken
   (or portions if preferred)
4 large potatoes, peeled and
   left whole
4 large onions, peeled
1 packet minestrone soup
400 ml water or meat stock
250 ml fresh or frozen peas

Place chicken into a cold potjie. Arrange potatoes and onions around chicken. Sprinkle soup powder over chicken and vegetables. Heat water or stock in a smaller potjie and pour over chicken. Cover and simmer slowly for 1¹/₂ hours. Baste chicken with juices every 30 minutes. Add peas during last 15 minutes of cooking time. Add more water or stock during cooking if necessary.
Serves 4

Spiced chicken with yoghurt

Beatrice's chicken pot
Potjie No. 2

12 chicken thighs
15 ml cooking oil
3 large onions, sliced
baby potatoes
baby carrots
green beans, sliced
125 ml chutney
150 ml cream
75 ml mayonnaise
1 packet onion soup
15 ml soy sauce
200 ml grated Cheddar cheese
350 g mushrooms, sliced

Brown chicken pieces in heated cooking oil in potjie, remove and set aside. Sauté onion until transparent, then replace chicken on top of onions. Arrange potatoes, carrots and beans on top of chicken. Mix chutney, half the cream, the mayonnaise and onion soup powder and pour over vegetable layer. Cover with lid and allow to simmer gently for 1 hour or until chicken is almost tender. Add soy sauce, remaining cream, cheese and mushrooms. Cover with lid and simmer for a further 15 minutes until cheese has melted.
Serves 6

Turkey potjie

Potjie No. 3 or 4

3 kg turkey, cut into portions
25 g butter
60 ml cooking oil
500 g bacon, cut into strips
4 large onions, cut into rings
5 cloves garlic, chopped
300 g mushrooms, sliced
1 green pepper, seeded and
    sliced
250 ml late harvest wine
freshly ground black pepper
    to taste
15 ml mustard powder
2 sprigs fresh rosemary
50 ml fresh thyme
8 whole cloves
60 ml soy sauce
juice of 1 lemon
10 medium potatoes, halved
1 pineapple, cubed
4 stalks celery
8 medium carrots
500 g baby marrows
500 ml fresh or frozen peas

Heat butter and oil in potjie, add turkey pieces and brown on all sides. Add bacon and fry until crisp. Add onion, garlic, mushrooms and green pepper and sauté until onion is transparent. Heat wine and remaining ingredients, except vegetables, and pour over turkey. Cover with lid and simmer slowly for 1–1½ hours. Arrange potatoes on top of turkey, followed by layers of pineapple, celery, carrots, baby marrow and finally peas. Replace lid and simmer gently for another hour. Just before serving, stir potjie gently. Remove whole spices and serve with rice or Stampkoring (page 79).
Serves 8

Duck or chicken with gooseberries and port

Potjie No. 3

1 duck or chicken,
    cut into portions
15 ml butter
15 ml cooking oil
4 spring onions, or 1 onion,
    cut into rings
1 x 410 g can Cape
    gooseberries, drained
30 ml brown sugar or smooth
    apricot jam
30 ml white wine vinegar
juice of 1 lemon
15 ml cornflour
100 ml port or hanepoot wine

Heat butter and oil in potjie. Add chicken or duck and brown on all sides. Add onion and sauté until transparent. Add remaining ingredients and cover with lid. Simmer for 1–1½ hours or until duck or chicken is tender.
Serves 6

Attie Botha's chicken potjie

Potjie No. 2 or 3

1 kg chicken breasts
15 ml cooking oil
7–10 ml salt
freshly ground black pepper
    to taste
a little cake flour
2 medium onions, chopped
1 clove garlic, crushed
500–750 ml chicken stock
200 g uncooked rice
400 g fresh or 1 x 410 g can
    waterblommetjies
300 g mushrooms, thinly
    sliced
500 g fresh or frozen mixed
    vegetables

Cut chicken off bone and cube. Use bones to make stock. Heat oil in potjie and brown chicken. Sprinkle salt, pepper and flour over chicken. Add onion and garlic and sauté until transparent. Add a little stock and cover. Simmer for about 10 minutes. Do not allow to boil dry and add more stock if necessary. Add rice, top with more stock and simmer for a further 30 minutes or until rice is just tender. If necessary, add more heated stock. Arrange waterblommetjies on top of the rice, then mushrooms. If using fresh vegetables, add now, but if using frozen vegetables, only add later. Cover and simmer for a further 15 minutes or until vegetables are cooked but still crispy. If using frozen vegetables, add now and allow to cook for 5 minutes. Stir potjie carefully before serving.
Serves 4–6

Chicken and banana in a potjie

Potjie No. 2

10 chicken thighs or
    drumsticks
15 ml butter
15 ml cooking oil
1 onion, chopped
1 clove garlic, crushed
15 ml curry powder
15 ml lemon juice or vinegar
15 ml smooth apricot jam or
    chutney
250 ml chicken stock
5 ml salt
freshly ground black pepper
    to taste
1 bay leaf
1 small piece chilli or
    1 ml cayenne pepper
4 ripe bananas, peeled and
    sliced
50 g blanched almond flakes
    (optional)

Heat butter and oil in potjie, add chicken and brown on all sides. Add onion and garlic and sauté until transparent. Add curry and fry for a few seconds. Heat lemon juice or vinegar, jam or chutney and stock. Add to chicken together with salt, pepper, bay leaf and chilli or cayenne. Cover and simmer slowly for 1–1½ hours or until chicken is tender. Arrange banana on top. Sprinkle with almonds, replace lid and simmer for 10 minutes or until banana is soft. Serve with rice, lentils and a sambal.
Serves 6

Delightful duck
Potjie Nos. 1 and 2

1 duck, cut into portions
1 small pork fillet (optional)
15 ml butter
15 ml cooking oil
300 ml dry white wine
150 ml chicken stock
5 ml salt
freshly ground black pepper
   to taste
vegetables in season (baby
   potatoes, carrots and mealies,
   pickling onions, fresh or
   frozen peas, asparagus)
250 ml orange juice
5 ml cornflour

Heat potjie, add butter and oil and brown duck and pork fillet. In a smaller potjie heat wine, stock, salt and pepper. Add to duck. Cover with lid and simmer slowly for 1½ hours or until duck is almost cooked. Arrange potatoes, onions, carrots, peas and other vegetables in season on top of duck. Replace lid and simmer for a further 15 minutes or until the vegetables are cooked but still crispy. Mix orange juice and cornflour and add to the vegetables. Simmer for another 10 minutes. Stir the potjie carefully and serve with rice and a mixed salad.
Serves 6

Turkey in red wine
Potjie Nos. 1 and 4

1 x 4 kg turkey, cut into portions
125 g rindless bacon, chopped
50 g butter
1 large onion, chopped
3 cloves garlic, chopped
50 ml brandy
10 ml salt
freshly ground black pepper
   to taste
350 ml dry red wine
350 ml chicken stock
1 bouquet garni (sprig fresh
   rosemary, sprig fresh parsley,
   1 stalk celery, bay leaf, sprig
   fresh thyme)
500 g button mushrooms
2 baby marrows, sliced
2 large carrots, chopped
30 ml chopped fresh parsley
   or 10 ml dried

Heat potjie and fry bacon until crisp. Remove and set aside. Add butter to bacon fat already in the potjie, add turkey pieces a few at a time and brown. Add a little more butter if necessary. Add onion and garlic and fry until transparent. Heat brandy over fire in a ladle or small metal container. Be careful that the brandy does not come into direct contact with the flames. Set alight and pour flaming brandy over turkey. As soon as the flames die down, season turkey with salt and pepper. Heat wine and stock in a smaller potjie and pour over turkey. Add bacon and bouquet garni. Cover with lid and simmer gently for 2 hours or until turkey is tender. Add vegetables and simmer for a further 30 minutes. Sprinkle with parsley. If using dried parsley, replace lid and allow to stand for 5 minutes so that parsley can absorb steam. Remove bouquet garni and serve with Stampkoring (page 79).
Serves 15

Chicken seafood potjie
Flat-bottomed Potjie No. 6

2 chicken stock cubes
750 ml boiling water
5 ml mild curry powder
5 ml salt
freshly ground black pepper
   to taste
5 ml dried thyme
5 ml dried basil
125 ml cooking oil
1 medium onion, chopped
2 cloves garlic, chopped
8 chicken breasts, cubed
250 g frozen stir-fry mix
   (comprising mushrooms,
   peas, leeks and green
   peppers)
250 ml dry white wine
250 g parboiled rice
1 large can black mussels
   in shells, drained
250 g prawns, cleaned

Prepare a medium coal fire or make a small wood fire. Use a No. 6 flat-bottomed potjie with a stand or have grid ready on fire for potjie. Mix stock cubes, boiling water, curry powder, salt, pepper and herbs in separate potjie. Heat oil in flat-bottomed potjie and sauté onion and garlic until transparent. Add chicken and fry until golden brown. Add half the stock, cover with lid and allow to simmer for 35 minutes. Place stir-fry mixture on top of chicken. Pour a little of the stock mixture over chicken. If necessary, sprinkle a little of the wine over. Replace lid and simmer for another 15 minutes. Place rice, mussels and prawns on top of chicken. Pour wine over, replace lid and simmer for 15 minutes or until prawns are done and mussels heated through. Just before serving, stir potjie carefully. Serve with garlic bread.
Serves 6

Chicken and dumplings
Potjie Nos. 1 and 3

1 Cornish hen, about 2 kg
15 ml cooking oil or piece of
   chicken fat
15 ml butter
1 onion, chopped
10 ml salt
freshly ground black pepper
   to taste
2 whole cloves
1 bay leaf
4 whole allspice
6 black peppercorns
1 blade mace or a little
   grated nutmeg
4 small carrots, scraped
4 leeks, chopped or
   6 spring onions
500 ml chicken stock or
   250 ml chicken stock and
   250 ml dry white wine
15 ml lemon juice

PARSLEY DUMPLINGS
250 ml cake flour
2 ml salt
10 ml baking powder
60 ml chopped fresh parsley
   or 20 ml dried
15 ml chicken fat (can be
   spooned off pot and cooled)
   or 15 ml cooking oil
200 ml milk, or half milk half
   water

Wash hen thoroughly under cold running water. Tie wings and legs into position. Heat oil and butter in potjie and brown hen on all sides. Add onion and sauté until transparent. Season hen with salt and pepper. Add remaining spices to potjie and arrange vegetables around hen. Heat liquid in smaller potjie. Add to hen. Cover with lid and simmer slowly for 1½–2 hours or until hen is almost tender. Check liquid and add more if necessary as the dumplings will absorb a lot of the liquid.

To prepare the dumplings, sift dry ingredients, add parsley and mix well. Add oil or fat and stir in milk to form a soft dough. Arrange dumplings around the hen and replace lid. Simmer for 20–25 minutes until dumplings are cooked. Do not peep into the potjie during the cooking process otherwise the dumplings will collapse.
Serves 6

Variation
Substitute dried or fresh mixed herbs for parsley.

Hint
Save a little liquid from the potjie to serve separately as gravy.

Chutney chicken potjie
Potjie No. 2

15 ml butter
2 onions, chopped
250 ml vinegar
125 ml chutney
30 ml Worcestershire sauce
10 ml sugar
5 ml curry powder
5 ml salt
1 ml turmeric
1 x 1.5 kg chicken, cut into
   portions
1 x 500 g packet frozen mixed
   vegetables

Heat butter in potjie, add onion and sauté until transparent. Set aside. Mix half the sautéed onion with the vinegar, chutney, Worcestershire sauce, sugar, curry powder, salt and turmeric. Place chicken pieces into this sauce and marinate for 1 hour. Arrange marinated chicken pieces on top of remaining onion in potjie. Pour marinade over chicken, cover with lid and simmer slowly for about 1 hour. Remove lid, add frozen vegetables, replace lid and simmer for 10–15 minutes until the vegetables are just cooked. Serve with rice.
Serves 4–6

Chicken and dumplings

Eastern Delights

Chicken curry in a potjie

Potjie No. 2 or 3

9 chicken thighs or drumsticks
   (about 1 kg)
15 ml cooking oil
15 ml butter
2 onions, cut into rings
3 cloves garlic, crushed
5 cardamom pods
1 stick cinnamon
1 bay leaf
30 ml chopped root ginger
1 small piece chilli, chopped
15 ml mild curry powder
2 ml turmeric
5 ml ground coriander
3 whole cloves
1 x 410 g can whole tomatoes,
   chopped or 3 large
   tomatoes, skinned and
   chopped
6 medium potatoes, peeled
5 ml salt
a few curry leaves (optional)

Heat oil and butter in potjie and brown chicken a few pieces at a time. Remove and set aside. Add onion to left over oil in potjie and sauté until transparent. Grind garlic, cardamom, cinnamon, bay leaf, ginger, chilli, curry powder, turmeric, coriander and cloves into a paste with a pestle and mortar. Add this mixture to onion and fry gently for 2 minutes. Place chicken on top of onions and then top with tomatoes. Arrange potatoes on top of tomatoes and sprinkle with salt and curry leaves. Cover with lid and simmer gently for 1–1½ hours or until chicken and potatoes are tender. Serve with rice and Cucumber sambal (this page).
Serves 6

Lamb curry with apricots and sultanas

Potjie No. 2 or 3

1 kg boneless thick rib of
   lamb, cubed
250 ml sour cream
125 ml meat stock
15 ml garam masala
15 ml medium curry powder
30 ml ghee or 15 ml butter
   and 15 ml cooking oil
2 large onions, chopped
4 cloves garlic, chopped
1 piece root ginger, peeled
   and chopped
125 g sultanas
125 g dried apricots
7 ml salt
pepper to taste
30 ml lemon juice

Mix sour cream, meat stock, masala and curry powder. Place meat in glass or enamel bowl and pour this mixture over meat and allow to marinate in refrigerator for 4–6 hours.

Heat ghee or butter and oil and sauté onion, garlic and ginger until onion is transparent. Add meat plus the marinade, cover with lid and simmer for 50–60 minutes. Arrange sultanas and apricots on top of meat, replace lid and simmer for a further 15 minutes. Add salt, pepper and lemon juice and stir carefully until all ingredients are well mixed. Serve with rice and chutney.
Serves 6

Sambals

Sambal is the Malayan word for side dish. Any number of different sambals can be served in small amounts in small dishes with any curry.

BANANA AND COCONUT SAMBAL

3 bananas, sliced
15 ml lemon juice
pinch of salt
pinch of sugar
30 ml grated fresh desiccated
   coconut
½ chilli, seeded and finely
   chopped

Mix all the ingredients together and chill.

BANANA SAMBAL

4 bananas
natural yoghurt or milk

Peel and slice bananas. Cover with natural yoghurt or milk and chill.

CUCUMBER SAMBAL

100 ml chopped English
   cucumber
50 ml desiccated coconut
100 ml natural yoghurt
30 ml flaked almonds
15 ml lemon juice
15 ml chopped fresh mint
2 ml salt
pinch of freshly ground black
   pepper

Mix all the ingredients together and chill.

Clockwise from left: Lamb curry with apricots and sultanas, Chicken curry in a potjie, Chapatis, Baked bananas, Tomato sambal (page 79), Cucumber sambal, Banana and coconut sambal

Quince sambal

3 quinces, chopped or grated
15 ml lemon juice
1 small onion, chopped
1 green chilli, seeded and
   chopped
1 ml salt

Mix all the ingredients together and chill.

Other popular sambals

Mix 250 g cottage cheese with
   30 ml desiccated coconut
Pineapple chunks
Chopped tomatoes, mixed
   with chopped onion, fresh
   coriander leaves or parsley,
   salt, black pepper and a
   small piece of red chilli,
   seeded and chopped
Chopped prunes in natural
   yoghurt
Toasted coconut or raisins or
   almonds

Baked bananas in a potjie
Flat-bottomed Potjie No. 3

To round off the meal, try this simple but delicious dessert.

6 bananas
50 ml cream
30 ml honey
5 ml ground cinnamon

Pull a small piece of peel off the banana without taking it off altogether. Spoon a little cream and honey into each banana and sprinkle with cinnamon. Place bananas open side up on the bottom of greased potjie. Heat slowly and bake bananas for 15–20 minutes or until soft.
Serves 6

Note: The bananas can also be wrapped up in aluminium foil (shiny side inside) and grilled over the coals.

Chapati in a potjie
Flat-bottomed Potjie No. 3

Chapatis are flat, unleavened pancakes made from whole-wheat flour. The secret to good chapatis is to fry them and eat them within half an hour. Cooked chapatis will stay fresh longer if covered with a warm cloth to prevent the moisture from evaporating.

500 g whole-wheat flour
2 ml salt
50 ml butter
± 250 ml water

Mix the flour and salt together. Cut butter into smaller pieces and rub into the flour with your fingertips. Gradually add enough water to make a soft dough. Knead the dough for 5 minutes until it becomes elastic. Cover the dough and place in refrigerator for 2–3 hours. Pinch off pieces of the dough and mould them into balls the size of an egg. On a floured board, roll each ball into a 180 mm round – the thickness of a pancake. Gently heat a greased flat-bottomed potjie and place a round of dough in it. Fry for 2 minutes on each side. Remove. Brush both sides with a little melted ghee or butter and fry to a light brown colour.

Fish

Rice and seafood potjie
Potjie Nos. 1 and 2

        250 g each of the following fish:
            squid, cleaned and cut into rings
            prawns, deveined and shelled
            monkfish, cut into pieces
            fresh or canned mussels, with shell
            kabeljou fillets
        30 ml olive oil
        2 onions, chopped
        2 cloves garlic, chopped
        1 x 410 g can tomatoes, coarsely chopped
        15 ml fresh oregano or 5 ml dried
        15 ml chopped fresh parsley or 5 ml dried
        7 ml salt
        white pepper to taste
        500 g uncooked rice
        2 litres fish stock

Heat oil in potjie. Add fish, a few pieces at a time and fry to a golden brown. Add onion and garlic and sauté until transparent. Add tomato, herbs and seasonings and simmer for a few minutes. Spoon rice on top of fish. Heat stock in smaller potjie and pour over rice. Cover with lid and simmer slowly for $^3/_4$–1 hour or until the liquid has been absorbed.
Serves 10

Rice and seafood potjie

Yellowtail potjie

Potjie No. 3

1.5 kg yellowtail, sliced into
    portions
2 large onions, sliced
50 ml cooking oil or a mixture
    of butter and oil
3 large ripe tomatoes, skinned
    and chopped
5 ml salt
freshly ground black pepper
    to taste
5 ml chopped fresh thyme or
    2 ml dried
½ cabbage, shredded
    (broccoli or cauliflower can
    also be used)
3 stalks leafy celery, chopped
500 g fresh green beans, cut
    into pieces
6 carrots, coarsely grated
extra butter

Sauté onion in heated oil or mixture of oil
and butter until transparent. Add tomato,
salt, pepper and thyme and simmer to a
pulp. Add vegetables to tomato mixture.
Stir very well so that vegetables are well
coated with tomato. Place fish on top of
vegetables. Dot with more butter. Cover
with lid and simmer slowly for about
45 minutes or until the fish is cooked.
Serve with Herby potbrood (page 84).
Serves 8

Fish and potato potjie

Potjie Nos. ³/₄ or 1, and 2 or 3

1 kg kingklip fillets, cut into
    portions
2 large onions, sliced
3–4 cloves garlic, crushed
30 ml olive or cooking oil
500 g potatoes, thinly sliced
15 ml chopped fresh dill
    or 5 ml dried
50 ml chopped fresh parsley
    or 20 ml dried
7 ml salt
freshly ground black pepper
    to taste
lemon juice to taste
250 ml milk or thin cream
250 ml fish stock
30 ml butter

Sauté onion and garlic in heated oil in the
larger potjie. Remove and set aside.
Arrange half the potato in bottom of
potjie, sprinkle with half the sautéed
onion mixture. Combine the dill, parsley,
salt and pepper. Season onion with a third
of the seasoning. Place fish fillets on top,
sprinkle with lemon juice and a third
of the seasoning. Arrange remaining
potato on top of fish and sprinkle with
remaining onion and seasoning. Heat
milk or cream and fish stock in a smaller
potjie. Pour over fish and potato. Dot with
butter, cover with lid and simmer very
slowly over a small fire for 30–45 minutes
or until potato is cooked.
Serves 6

Variation
*A few cleaned prawns or canned
prawns may be placed on top of
fish. If using canned prawns use
the prawn juice in place of some
of the fish stock.*

Fish under a lid

Potjie Nos. 1 and 3

1.2 kg mixed fish (squid,
    kingklip, kabeljou, red roman
    or white steenbras)
6 slices French bread
50 ml chopped fresh parsley

TOMATO SAUCE
50 ml olive oil
1 onion, chopped
2 cloves garlic, chopped
½ red Spanish sweet pepper,
    seeded and chopped
1 x 410 g can tomatoes,
    chopped or 4 large
    tomatoes, skinned and
    chopped
100 ml dry white wine
10 ml salt
freshly ground black pepper
    to taste

LEMON BUTTER
50 ml butter
5 ml lemon juice
5 ml grated lemon rind

First prepare the tomato sauce separately
in the smaller potjie. Heat half the oil, add
onion, garlic and red pepper and sauté
until transparent. Add tomato, wine, salt
and pepper. Cover with lid and simmer
until sauce has thickened.

Pour remaining oil into larger potjie
and heat. Add fish a few pieces at a time
and fry until golden brown. Pour slightly
thickened tomato sauce over fish. Cover
and simmer gently for about 15 minutes.

To prepare lemon butter, soften butter
with fork and blend in lemon juice and
rind. Spread bread with lemon butter,
then arrange bread slices on top of fish,
buttered-side under. Replace lid and
allow to simmer for about 5 minutes.
Sprinkle with parsley and serve.
Serves 6

From left to right: Potjie smoorsnoek, Fish under a lid

Potjie smoorsnoek
Potjie No. 3

1 kg salted (or smoked) snoek
60 ml cooking oil or 30 ml butter
   and 30 ml cooking oil
2–3 large onions, sliced
6 medium potatoes, thickly sliced
500 g tomatoes, skinned and coarsely chopped
1 small chilli, seeded and chopped
1 small bunch sorrel or 15 ml lemon juice

Cover snoek with cold water. Soak for a few hours or overnight depending on how salty the snoek is. Discard the water and coarsely flake fish, discarding bones. Heat oil or butter and oil in potjie, add onions and sauté until golden brown. Remove onion and set aside. Place potato slices on the bottom of the potjie. Spoon onion on top and follow with flaked fish. Spoon tomato and remaining ingredients over. Cover with lid and simmer slowly for 30–45 minutes or until potatoes are tender and the fish is cooked. Serve with rice.
Serves 6

Mussel potjie

Potjie No. 2

50 black mussels
1 medium onion, finely
   chopped
2 cloves garlic, finely chopped
30 g butter
50 ml chopped fresh parsley
250 ml dry white wine
2 ml salt
freshly ground black pepper
   to taste
100 ml fresh cream

Soak mussels in fresh, cold water for 30 minutes. Scrub shells clean and pull off the beard. Sauté onion and garlic in heated butter in potjie until transparent. Add parsley, heated wine, salt and pepper. Simmer for a few minutes. Add cleaned mussels, cover with lid and simmer for about 5 minutes until the mussels have opened. Discard any mussels that have failed to open. Add cream and heat through. Sprinkle with more chopped parsley and serve with Potbrood (page 84).
Serves 6

Hint
Canned or frozen mussels may be used instead of fresh. When using canned mussels, add the juice to the potjie as well.

Note: When gathering mussels yourself, it is best first to seek advice from the Department of Sea Fisheries, as a 'red tide' will render the mussels unsafe to eat.

Perlemoen and wine casserole

Potjie Nos. 1 and 3

2 medium perlemoen
30 ml cooking oil or
   15 ml butter and
   15 ml cooking oil
4 rashers bacon, rind
   removed and coarsely
   chopped
1 large onion, thinly sliced
1 clove garlic, crushed
250 ml dry white wine
15 ml lemon juice
30 ml chopped fresh parsley
   or 10 ml dried
5 ml salt
white pepper to taste
pinch of grated nutmeg
1 bay or lemon leaf

Cut perlemoen across in 5 mm thick slices. Pound lightly with a mallet and halve slices. Fry perlemoen lightly in heated oil or butter and oil in large potjie. Add bacon and fry until crisp. Add onion and garlic and sauté until onion is transparent. Heat wine and lemon juice in smaller potjie and add to the perlemoen with the remaining ingredients. Cover with lid and simmer slowly until perlemoen is tender, about 1½ hours. Sprinkle extra parsley over to garnish. Serve with rice or Potbrood (page 84).
Serves 4

Natal fish curry

Potjie Nos. 1 and 3

1 kg firm fish (kingklip,
   yellowtail or kabeljou),
   cut into portions
75 ml cooking oil
2 brinjals, thinly sliced
1 large onion, sliced
2 cloves garlic, chopped
15 ml chopped root ginger
15 ml mild curry powder
5 ml turmeric
15 ml ground coriander
2 ml cumin
2 ml ground aniseed
1 small piece chilli
30 ml tamarind
250 ml fish stock
7 ml salt

Brush the larger potjie with oil and heat to smoking. Brush brinjal with oil and place in potjie to 'grill' to a golden brown on both sides. Remove brinjal and set aside while preparing the curry sauce. Heat remaining oil in a smaller potjie. Add onion and garlic and sauté until transparent. Add ginger, curry powder, turmeric, coriander, cumin, aniseed and chilli and sauté for a few minutes. In the meantime, soften tamarind in heated fish stock. Add to the fried spices and simmer for a few minutes. Return brinjal to a larger potjie and arrange fish portions on top of brinjal. Season with salt. Pour curry sauce over fish and simmer slowly over a small fire for 20–30 minutes or until the fish is cooked. Serve with banana salad, Potbrood (page 84) or rice.
Serves 6

Prawn and banana curry

Potjie No. 3

500 g prawns
30 ml cooking oil
1 large onion, chopped
1 clove garlic, chopped
1 green pepper, seeded and
   cut into strips
5 ml turmeric
5 ml salt
1 ml cayenne pepper (optional)
5 ml ground coriander
5 ml cumin
2 ml garam masala
250 ml milk
4 bananas

Shell and devein prawns and rinse well in cold water. Dry prawns on paper towelling. Heat oil in potjie and lightly fry prawns. Add onion, garlic and green pepper and sauté until transparent. Add remaining ingredients, except milk and banana, and fry lightly for a few minutes. Pour warm milk over fish, cover with lid and simmer slowly for 15–20 minutes or until fish is cooked. Slice bananas and arrange on top of fish. Replace lid and simmer for another 5 minutes until banana is soft.
Serves 6

Sweet-sour fish with vegetables

Potjie No. 2

1 kg firm fish fillets
30 ml cooking oil
2 medium onions, sliced
125 g mushrooms, sliced
1 carrot, cut into strips
½ green pepper, seeded and
   cut into strips
30 ml soy sauce
15 ml tomato paste
50 ml wine vinegar
15 ml cornflour
125 ml fish stock

Heat oil in potjie, add onion, mushrooms, carrot and green pepper and sauté until onion is transparent. Arrange fish on top of vegetables. Mix soy sauce, tomato paste, wine vinegar, cornflour and fish stock together and add to fish. Cover with lid and simmer slowly for 15 minutes or until the fish is cooked.
Serves 6

Cape tuna potjie

Potjie Nos. 1 and 3

1 kg fresh tuna steaks
   (20 mm thick)
50 ml olive oil
1 medium onion, chopped
2 cloves garlic, crushed
30 ml sultanas
125 ml dry white wine
4 tomatoes, skinned and
   chopped or 1 x 410 g can
   tomatoes, chopped
4 medium potatoes, thinly
   sliced
5 ml salt
freshly ground black pepper
   to taste
200 g black olives, stoned
15 ml almonds (optional)
10 ml capers

Heat oil in larger potjie. Lightly fry tuna steaks a few at a time. Add onion and garlic and sauté until transparent. In the meantime, soak sultanas in wine and allow to stand until swollen. Heat wine and sultanas in smaller potjie and add to fish. Add tomato. Arrange potato slices on top of fish and season with salt and pepper. Sprinkle olives, almonds (if using) and capers over fish. Cover with lid and simmer slowly for 30–40 minutes or until fish and potatoes are cooked. Add a little fish stock if necessary.
Serves 6

Fish, spinach and mushroom potjie
Potjie No. 3

500 g fresh or frozen stock
   fish (hake) fillets, cut into
   portions
500 g smoked haddock fillets,
   cut into portions
30 ml cooking oil
30 ml butter
1 onion, chopped
500 g fresh or frozen spinach
500 g button mushrooms
15 ml chopped fresh oregano
   or 5 ml dried
30 ml chopped fresh parsley
   or 10 ml dried
10 ml salt
freshly ground black pepper
   to taste
500 g potatoes, thinly sliced
30 ml lemon juice
250 ml cream
250 ml fish stock or
   dry white wine
150 ml grated Cheddar
   cheese

Heat butter and oil in potjie and sauté onion until transparent, then remove and set aside. If using fresh spinach, rinse thoroughly in cold water. Discard stalks and chop leaves coarsely. Meanwhile, place mushrooms in heated butter and oil and sauté for a few minutes, then remove and set aside. Mix herbs, salt and pepper. Arrange ingredients in potjie starting with potato. Sprinkle with a little seasoning mixture followed by the sautéed onion. Arrange hake fillets on top. Sprinkle with a little lemon juice. Spoon spinach on top of fish and follow with haddock fillets. Sprinkle fish with remaining lemon juice. Place mushrooms on top of haddock and sprinkle with

Fish, spinach and mushroom potjie

remaining seasoning mixture. Pour heated cream and stock or wine over. Cover with lid and simmer very slowly for 30–45 minutes until potato is cooked. Sprinkle with cheese, replace lid and simmer for a further 10 minutes or until cheese has melted. To produce a golden-brown top, place a few small coals on top of the lid.

Serves 6

Onion and hake potjie
Potjie No. 2

500 g hake, cut into portions
500 g onions, thinly sliced
60 g butter
5 ml salt
freshly ground black pepper
   to taste
5 ml grated lemon rind
juice of ½ lemon
125 g Cheddar cheese,
   cut into 10 mm cubes
60 ml dry white wine
15 ml chopped fresh mixed
   herbs or 5 ml dried
30 ml chopped fresh parsley

Melt butter in potjie, add onions and sauté until soft and transparent. Arrange fish on top of onions. Season fish with salt and pepper. Add lemon rind and juice. Sprinkle cheese cubes over fish. Pour heated wine into potjie and sprinkle mixed herbs over. Cover potjie and cook gently over coals for 30 minutes. (Hot coals placed on top of the lid during cooking will ensure a nice brown top.) Sprinkle with chopped parsley and serve.

Serves 4

Perlemoen on the coals
Flat-bottomed Potjie

1 perlemoen
15 ml butter
salt and freshly ground black
   pepper to taste
5 button mushrooms, sliced
15 ml grated Cheddar cheese
2 rashers bacon
30 ml chopped fresh parsley

Cut perlemoen from shell, remove viscera and scrub clean. Gently pound perlemoen until limp. Place half the butter on a piece of foil, shiny side up. Place perlemoen on top of butter and season well. Arrange mushrooms and cheese on top, then bacon. Dot with remaining butter and sprinkle parsley over. Fold foil over to make a parcel, then place in potjie. Bake over a slow fire for about 1 hour. Remove from potjie, unwrap and serve with bread to mop up the juices.

Serves 2

Two oceans seafood potjie
Potjie No. 3

1 octopus
10 alikreukels
18 white mussels
18 black mussels
2 crayfish
1 kg musselcracker or yellowtail
2 onions, sliced
15 ml cooking oil or olive oil
250 ml uncooked rice
5 ml grated lemon rind
30 ml fresh dill or 10 ml dried
fish stock
salt to taste
freshly ground black pepper
   to taste
chopped fresh parsley

Prepare seafood as follows:

Octopus: Beat the octopus on the rocks until it is limp. Drop it quickly into boiling water, then remove and pull off the skin. Slice legs into rings and set aside.

Alikreukel: Boil alikreukel in the shell in boiling seawater for 20 minutes. Take them out of their shells and remove the trapdoor and viscera. Rinse well.

White mussels: Cover with fresh cold water and leave to soak for 30 minutes. Pour off water and repeat process 3 times until all the sand has been removed.

Black mussels: Scrub well with stiff brush and remove any seaweed. Cover with cold water and leave to soak for 30 minutes. Pour off water and repeat process at least 3 times to remove all the sand. Use only closed mussels, since damaged ones are not safe to eat.

Crayfish: Cook on the beach in seawater – 15 minutes from the time the water starts to boil. Cut the crayfish, claws and all, in half, remove intestinal vein and set aside.

Musselcracker or yellowtail: Fillet fish, remove skin and cut into portions. Use head and bones to make stock in smaller potjie. Strain stock and set aside until required.

Prepare potjie as follows: Sauté onion in the heated cooking or olive oil. Add rice, lemon rind and dill and sauté for a minute or two. Add enough stock to cover rice completely. Arrange fish in potjie starting with the octopus, followed by the alikreukel. Simmer for approximately 10 minutes. Now arrange musselcracker or yellowtail portions on top. Follow with the crayfish halves and finally all the mussels. Cover with lid and simmer for approximately 10 minutes or until all the shells have opened. Remove all unopened shells and discard. Season to taste with salt and pepper. Cover with lid and heat through for a few minutes. Sprinkle with chopped parsley and serve.

Serves 6

Crayfish and kingklip potjie

Potjie No. 3 or 4

This recipe is based on a Greek fish and vegetable casserole.

3 cooked crayfish
600 g kingklip fillets, cubed
50 g butter
1 onion, chopped
2 cloves garlic, crushed
50 ml brandy
½ each yellow, red and green
   pepper, seeded and diced
300 g brown mushrooms, sliced
3 tomatoes, skinned and
   chopped
250 g baby marrows,
   sliced into rings
10 ml chopped fresh basil
   or 2 ml dried
30 ml chopped fresh oregano
   or 10 ml dried
2 ml sugar
salt and freshly ground black
   pepper to taste
250 ml dry white wine
50 ml cake flour (if necessary)
40 g butter (if necessary)
125 ml black olives
200 g Feta cheese, crumbled

Split cooked crayfish down the centre, remove dark vein and take the flesh out of the shell and cube. Save the legs to use in the potjie as well. Heat butter in potjie and sauté onion and garlic until transparent. Add crayfish and kingklip. Heat brandy carefully in a soup ladle and set alight. Pour flaming brandy over the fish. Add diced peppers, followed by mushrooms, tomato and baby marrows. Sprinkle fish and vegetables with basil, 10 ml of the fresh oregano or 2 ml dried, sugar, salt and pepper. Heat wine in a smaller potjie and add to the vegetables and fish. Cover with lid and simmer slowly for 30 minutes or until the fish is cooked. Mix the flour and butter to a paste. Drop small pieces of this mixture into the potjie to thicken juices if necessary. Add black olives and sprinkle with cheese. Finally sprinkle over remaining oregano. Serve with Potbrood (page 84).
Serves 6

Steamed crayfish

Flat-bottomed Potjie No. 3 and Potjie No. 1

1 crayfish per person
seawater or salt water

GARLIC-LEMON-BUTTER SAUCE

100 g butter
2 cloves garlic, crushed
100 ml cooking oil
50 ml lemon juice
2 ml salt
white pepper to taste

Split crayfish and remove alimentary canal. Add water to potjie to a depth of 25 mm. Place a rack or a bed of straw in the bottom of the potjie. Arrange crayfish halves, shell-side down, on rack or bed of straw. Cover with lid, bring to the boil, reduce heat and steam for 15–20 minutes.

To make the sauce, melt butter slowly in smaller potjie, removing scum that is formed. Add garlic and fry for a few minutes. Add remaining ingredients and simmer for a few more minutes. Serve piping hot with steamed crayfish.

Fish biriani

Potjie No. 3

A very popular dish with the Cape Malay and Indian communities.

1 kg firm fish fillets (use any
   firm fish such as kingklip
   or snoek)
cooking oil for frying
10 ml salt
4 large onions, thinly sliced
8 cloves garlic, crushed
1 stick cinnamon
2 whole cloves
4 green chillies (or less for
   a more delicate flavour)
5 cardamom pods
5 ml turmeric
5 ml cumin seeds
2 ml fennel seeds (optional)
1 small knob root ginger,
   chopped
3 medium tomatoes, skinned
   and chopped
1 kg uncooked rice
2 threads saffron dissolved in
   250 ml boiling water

Heat oil in potjie. Season fish with a little salt and fry lightly until golden brown. Remove fish from oil and set aside. Add onion and garlic to potjie and sauté until transparent. Place all the spices and the ginger in a pestle and mortar and grind to form a fine masala. Add tomatoes and masala to sautéed onion and garlic and place fish fillets on top. Sprinkle rice and remaining salt over fish. Pour in saffron water. Cover with lid and simmer slowly for 1 hour or until the fish is cooked and most of the liquid has been absorbed. Add more boiling water if necessary. This dish should not be too dry.
Serves 10

Clockwise from left: Seafood starter, Crayfish and kingklip potjie, rice, Steamed crayfish

Seafood starter
Potjie No. 2

50 black mussels

1 crayfish

125 ml dry white wine

2 cloves garlic, finely chopped

freshly ground black pepper
   to taste

30 ml finely chopped fresh parsley

1 small tomato, skinned and diced

juice of ½ lemon

250 ml cream

Scrub mussels and stand in clean seawater for about 6 hours. Drain and rinse well in clean cold water. Cook crayfish in a little boiling water for 15–20 minutes. Twist off tail, remove vein and cut into 20 mm thick slices. Place mussels in potjie, add heated wine, garlic, pepper, parsley and tomato. Cover with lid and steam slowly for 15 minutes. Sprinkle with lemon juice and add crayfish. Steam for about 5 minutes. Add cream and heat through, but do not boil. Eat with chunks of bread to mop up juices.

Serves 6 as a starter or 4 as a main meal

Vegetables

Vegetable potjie with cheesy topping
Potjie No. 2

2 medium onions, chopped

50 g butter

6 medium potatoes, parboiled and thinly sliced

2 medium brinjals, peeled and cubed

250 ml baby marrows, sliced diagonally into rings

300 g mushrooms, sliced

50 ml chopped fresh parsley

30 ml chopped fresh oregano or 10 ml dried

4 medium tomatoes, skinned and chopped
   or 1 x 410 g can tomatoes, chopped

250 ml fresh breadcrumbs

250 ml grated Cheddar cheese

Sauté onion until transparent in heated butter. Remove onion and set aside. Arrange vegetables in potjie in layers as follows: first potatoes, then brinjals, baby marrows and finally mushrooms. Add a little sautéed onion, parsley and oregano between each layer. Pour tomato pulp over top of vegetables. Cover with lid and simmer very slowly over slow fire for 1 hour or until the vegetables are cooked. Do not stir or peep too often. Now sprinkle with breadcrumbs and cheese. Replace lid and put potjie back on the fire for 15 minutes or until the cheese has melted. For a golden-brown crust, place a few small coals on the lid.
Serves 6 as a main dish

Clockwise from top left: Stowepatats (page 76), Instant bean potjie (page 76), Vegetable potjie with cheesy topping

Instant bean potjie

Potjie No. 1

15 ml cooking oil
6 rashers rindless bacon,
   chopped
2 large onions, sliced
1 x 410 g can butter beans
1 x 410 g can red kidney beans
30 ml brown sugar
15 ml vinegar
5 ml prepared mustard

Heat oil in potjie, add bacon and fry until crisp. Add onion and sauté until transparent. Drain beans if necessary. Add beans and remaining ingredients to potjie. Cover with lid and simmer gently for 20 minutes or until the beans are heated through.
Serves 6–8 as a side dish

Green beans in the potjie

Potjie No. 1

60 ml olive oil
500 g green beans, cut
   diagonally into 10 mm slices
1 medium onion, chopped
1 green pepper, seeded and
   chopped
1 tomato, skinned and chopped
salt and freshly ground black
   pepper to taste
5 ml sugar
100 ml water

Put oil in potjie and arrange vegetables in layers, starting with beans and followed by onion, green pepper, tomato, salt and pepper. Sprinkle with sugar and pour boiling water over. Cover with lid and simmer gently over a medium fire for about 30 minutes or until the vegetables are done. Can also be served cold as a salad.
Serves 6 as a side dish

Layered potatoes

Flat-bottomed Potjie No. 3

10 medium potatoes, peeled
   and thinly sliced
1 large onion, chopped
50 ml chopped fresh parsley
6 spring onions, chopped
10 ml salt
freshly ground black pepper
   to taste
1 sprig fresh thyme or
   5 ml dried
250 ml chicken stock
250 ml low fat cream or
   sour cream
30 g butter
150 ml grated Cheddar cheese

Grease a flat-bottomed potjie with butter. Arrange the potatoes, onion, parsley, spring onions, salt, pepper and herbs in layers in the potjie, repeating layers until all ingredients have been used up. Pour heated stock and cream over the top and dot with butter. Cover with lid and place on a small, slow fire for 45–60 minutes or until the potatoes are soft. Sprinkle cheese over, replace lid and leave on fire for another 10 minutes or until the cheese has melted. Serve immediately.
Serves 8–10 as a side dish

Stowepatats
(Braised sweet potatoes)

Flat-bottomed Potjie No.4

1 kg sweet potatoes, sliced
50 g butter
75 ml brown sugar
1 stick cinnamon
15 ml chopped root ginger or
   5 ml ground ginger
1 small piece naartjie, orange
   or lemon peel
2 ml salt
125 ml orange juice

Grease potjie with butter. Arrange a layer of sweet potatoes in the base of the potjie, dot with a little butter and sprinkle with a little sugar. Repeat layers of sweet potato, sugar and butter. Place cinnamon stick, ginger and peel on top. Season with salt and pour orange juice over. Cover with lid and simmer over a small fire for 30–45 minutes or until the sweet potatoes are done and a syrupy sauce has formed.
Serves 6 as a side dish

Variation
Use 30 ml dry sherry and
100 ml water instead of
orange juice.

Old-fashioned sousboontjies

Potjie No. 2

250 g dried sugar beans
7 ml salt
50 ml brown sugar
100 ml wine vinegar
50 ml butter

Soak beans overnight or use this quick soaking method. Rinse beans under cold running water. Place in pot and cover with cold water. Bring to the boil and boil for 5 minutes. Remove from heat and allow beans to stand for 1 hour. Drain and rinse thoroughly under cold running water. Cover again with cold water and slowly bring to the boil, then simmer with lid on for 2–3 hours or until beans are soft, adding more boiling water if necessary. Make sure there is still a little liquid in the potjie once the beans are done. Mash a few beans. Add remaining ingredients and simmer for 10 minutes or until the flavours are well blended. Allow to cool, then serve cold as a salad or hot with braaied soutribbetjie or boerewors.
Serves 10–12 as a side dish

Potjie roast potatoes

Potjie No. 1

8 medium potatoes
750 ml cooking oil for frying
1–2 cloves garlic, crushed
1 sprig fresh rosemary
5 ml salt

Peel potatoes. Half fill potjie with water. Bring to the boil and add potatoes. Parboil potatoes over a medium fire for about 10 minutes. Discard water and dry potjie thoroughly. Pour in oil. Heat over a medium fire until oil starts to bubble. Add garlic and rosemary. Add potatoes and cook quickly until golden brown. Remove potatoes with a slotted spoon and drain on paper towelling. Season with salt and serve immediately.
Serves 6

Stywepap

Potjie No. 1

500 ml water
2 ml salt
375 ml mealie meal
15 ml butter

Bring water and salt to the boil. Add mealie meal and leave in potjie without stirring. With a wooden spoon, use a cutting and not a stirring motion to mix the mealie meal with the water. Cover with lid and allow to simmer for 20 minutes or until pap is cooked. Stir at short intervals to prevent pap from scorching and to give it a light texture. Stir in butter and serve with any potjiekos with a lot of gravy.
Serves 6

Note: Stywepap is not very well known nor is it popular in the Western Cape. Should non-pap-eaters visit you, rather serve Stampkoring (page 79), rice or Potbrood (pager 84) instead of stywepap.

Quick potato soup

Potjie No. 2

4 rashers rindless bacon,
    coarsely chopped
15 ml butter
2 medium onions, chopped
6 large potatoes, cubed
500 ml chicken stock
5–10 ml salt
freshly ground black pepper
    to taste
500 ml milk
5 ml prepared mustard
30 ml chopped fresh parsley
100 ml grated Cheddar cheese

Fry bacon until crisp in heated potjie. Add butter, then onion and potato, and sauté until onion is transparent. Add heated chicken stock, salt and pepper. Cover with lid and simmer for 30–40 minutes or until potato is soft. Add milk and simmer slowly for a further 10 minutes until well heated through. The potato can be mashed with a potato masher or fork, if desired. Stir in mustard and parsley and serve immediately. Sprinkle with a little grated Cheddar cheese if desired.
Serves 4–6

Dried bean curry

Potjie Nos. 1 or 2, and 3

250 ml haricot beans
2 large onions, chopped
1 clove garlic, chopped
15–30 ml butter
5 ml curry powder
1 bay leaf
5–7 ml salt
freshly ground black pepper
    to taste
250 g dried apricots or apples
    or 1 fresh quince
15 ml vinegar
250 ml meat stock or water

Place beans in smaller potjie. Cover with cold water and bring to the boil. Boil rapidly for 5 minutes. Remove potjie from fire and allow beans to soak for 1 hour. The beans can also be soaked in cold water overnight. Using the larger potjie, sauté onion and garlic in heated butter until transparent. Add curry powder and fry gently. Add remaining ingredients, including beans, and simmer slowly until beans are tender. Serve with rice.
Serves 6 as a main dish

Creamed sweetcorn bake

Flat-bottomed Potjie No. 3

750 ml whole kernel corn
    (fresh, canned or frozen)
30 g butter
1 onion, chopped
3 eggs
100 ml mayonnaise or cream
5 ml salt
freshly ground black pepper
    to taste
5 ml dry mustard
200 ml grated Cheddar cheese

If using fresh mealies, cut kernels off cob or if using canned mealies, drain. Melt butter in potjie, add onion and sauté until transparent. Beat eggs and remaining ingredients, except cheese, together. Mix egg, onion and mealies and spoon into greased potjie. Sprinkle with cheese. Cover with lid and place a few small coals on top of the lid to melt the cheese and become golden brown. Bake slowly over a small fire for 30–40 minutes or until set.
Serves 6 as a side dish

Garlic vegetable potjie

Potjie No. 3

1 butternut, unpeeled and
    sliced
12 baby potatoes, scrubbed
    or 4 large potatoes, peeled
    and quartered
3 carrots, cut into chunks
12 pickling onions, peeled
6 small gem squashes,
    unpeeled and quartered
6 baby marrows, halved
2 brinjals, unpeeled and sliced
6 whole mushrooms
any other available vegetables
    of your choice
at least 12 whole cloves garlic,
    unpeeled
salt and freshly ground black
    pepper to taste
50 g butter, melted
50 ml olive or cooking oil

Arrange vegetables in layers in potjie starting with the ones that take longest to cook: butternut, potatoes, carrots, onions, gem squash, baby marrow, brinjal and then mushrooms on top. Place garlic in between each layer of vegetables. Season each layer with salt and pepper. Sprinkle butter and oil over top of vegetables. Cover with lid and place potjie over a small fire for $1^1/_2$ hours or until vegetables are cooked but still crisp. It is not necessary to add any liquid as the vegetables produce their own.
Serves 6 as a main dish

Beans and pork shank in a potjie

Potjie No. 3

500 ml dried haricot beans
50 ml brown sugar
15 ml dry mustard
10 ml salt
freshly ground black pepper
    to taste
30 ml wine vinegar
1 bay leaf
1 pickled pork shank
1 onion stuck with 2 whole
    cloves

Soak beans as described in the Old-fashioned sousboontjies recipe (page 76). After the beans have been drained, place into potjie. Cover with cold water and bring slowly to the boil. Cover with lid and simmer for $1-1^1/_2$ hours or until the beans are soft. Add remaining ingredients, placing the pork shank and onion on top of beans. Replace lid and simmer for 1 hour or until the shank is tender. If there is still too much liquid, increase heat and cook quickly to reduce.
Serves 6 as a side dish

Variations
Add vegetables such as leeks,
chunks of celery, baby marrows
and baby carrots.
Add 1 clove garlic, chopped and
1 x 410 g can whole tomatoes,
chopped to the potjie.
Substitute 50 ml honey or
golden syrup for the sugar.
Substitute 500 g frankfurters
for the pork shank, but only
add 15 minutes before end
of cooking time.

Herbed mustard sauce

Potjie No. $^3/_4$

30 ml mustard powder
75 ml brown sugar
15 ml cake flour
250 ml white vinegar
4 eggs, beaten
5 ml salt
5 ml white pepper
5–10 ml dried mixed herbs

Combine ingredients in small potjie and mix well. Whisk continuously over gentle heat until thickened. Remove from heat and keep warm. Serve with pickled or smoked meats.
Makes 300 ml

Spatzle

Potjie No. 2

1.3 litres water
10 ml salt
5 ml cooking oil
350 ml cake flour
1 egg, beaten
butter

Bring 1 litre water, 5 ml salt and 5 ml cooking oil to the boil in the potjie. Sift dry ingredients into a mixing bowl and mix with egg and remaining water. Spread dough onto a small bread board with a spoon and then, using a spatula, scrape off pieces the size of walnuts into the boiling water. Cook for 1 minute, remove and spoon into a colander. Repeat until all the dough is used up. Dot spatzle with a few knobs of butter and fork through gently. Place colander over hot water to keep warm. Serve with any potjie.
Serves 6

Ratatouille in a potjie

Potjie Nos. 1 and 3

This recipe is based on the traditional French ratatouille recipe. The flavoursome tomato sauce forms a basis for a variety of dishes.

4 medium brinjals, sliced
1 green pepper
1 red Spanish sweet pepper
250 g baby marrows
350 g brown mushrooms
2 stalks leafy celery, cut into
   pieces

TOMATO SAUCE

30 ml olive or cooking oil
1 large onion, chopped
3 cloves garlic, chopped
2 x 410 g can whole peeled
   tomatoes or 8 medium
   tomatoes, skinned and
   chopped
50 ml chopped fresh parsley
15 ml chopped fresh basil
   or 5 ml dried
1 sprig fresh rosemary
   or 5 ml dried
1 sprig fresh thyme
   or 5 ml dried
1 bay leaf

First prepare tomato sauce: Heat oil in small potjie, add onion and garlic and sauté until transparent. Add tomatoes and herbs and simmer gently until sauce is thick. Stir sauce occasionally to avoid burning. If you like, a knob of butter may be stirred in when sauce is cooked.

To prepare vegetables: Place brinjal on a large board or into a large sieve. Sprinkle with salt and allow to stand for 30 minutes. Rinse off excess salt under cold water and dry brinjal thoroughly on paper towelling. Place brinjal on grid over glowing coals. Brush slices with a little extra cooking oil. Braai until lightly browned. Turn, brush with oil and braai underside. Remove from coals and set aside. Meanwhile, place whole peppers, without brushing with oil, onto grid or place onto a braai fork and hold in the flames. Do not worry if the peppers become black. Remove from fire and rub skins off with a rough towel, or pull skins off with fingers. This is a time-consuming process, but the delicious braai flavour that results is well worth the effort. Cut peppers in half, remove the seeds and cut into strips.

Arrange half the brinjal slices in the larger potjie, followed by a few spoonfuls of the tomato sauce. Now place half the peppers and baby marrows on top of the brinjal. Spoon some more tomato sauce on top, then place half the mushrooms and celery on top followed by more tomato sauce. Continue in this way with the remaining vegetables, making sure that each layer is well covered with tomato sauce. Bring slowly to the boil, then simmer over low coals for 45–60 minutes. Serve with Potbrood (page 84).
Serves 6

Stampkoring in the potjie

Potjie Nos. 1 and 2

200 g stampkoring
1 large onion, chopped
15 ml butter
15 ml cooking oil
1 litre water
5 ml salt
50 g seedless raisins
   (optional)

Heat butter and oil in larger potjie. Add onion and sauté until transparent. Add koring and stir until it is coated with oil. Heat water and salt to boiling point in smaller potjie then add together with raisins (if using) to koring. Cover with lid and simmer slowly for 40–45 minutes or until koring is cooked. Add more boiling water if necessary. Do not stir during cooking process. If desired, stir in a large knob of butter just before serving.
Serves 6 as a side dish

Tomato sambal

500 g tomatoes
1 large onion, chopped
1 large green pepper, seeded
   and chopped
1 small piece chilli, chopped
50 ml chopped fresh parsley
5 ml salt

Chop tomatoes finely, but do not drain. Combine all the ingredients, and chill. Serve with curry.
Makes about 300 ml

Buttered vegetable potjie
Potjie No. 3

250 g butter
3 large onions, sliced
20 baby potatoes, scrubbed
20 baby carrots, scrubbed
250 ml vegetable or chicken
   stock
2 medium brinjals, cubed
10 baby marrows, sliced
   diagonally
350 g mushrooms, sliced
750 ml fresh or frozen peas
salt and freshly ground black
   pepper to taste
20 ml chopped fresh basil or
   5 ml dried

Heat half the butter in the potjie, add onions and sauté until transparent. Add potatoes and carrots and sauté lightly. Pour in heated stock and simmer slowly with lid on for about 20 minutes or until the vegetables are almost tender. Arrange remaining vegetables in layers on top of the potatoes and carrots, starting with the brinjal, then baby marrows, followed by the mushrooms and finally the peas. Sprinkle each layer with a little salt, pepper and herbs. Dot each layer with a little of the remaining butter, reserving enough for the top. Cover with lid and simmer slowly for 15–20 minutes until the vegetables are cooked but still crisp. Serve as a vegetarian main dish with Whole-wheat potbread (opposite page) or with Stywepap (page 77).
Serves 8–10

Braaied mushrooms with garlic butter

500 g large brown
   mushrooms

GARLIC BUTTER
100 g unsalted butter
50 ml chopped fresh parsley
3 cloves garlic, chopped
10 ml lemon juice
2 ml salt
freshly ground black pepper
   to taste

Cream butter, add remaining ingredients and beat until creamy. Remove the stems from the mushrooms and wipe the mushrooms clean with paper towelling. Place mushrooms on a large sheet of aluminium foil, shiny side up. Place a little garlic butter on each mushroom, then fold foil around mushrooms to form a parcel. Place over coals for about 10 minutes or until the butter is melted and the mushrooms cooked. Alternatively, place the mushrooms with the garlic butter in a large flat-bottomed potjie and cook over low heat until the mushrooms are cooked. Serve with Whole-wheat potbread (opposite page) to mop up the juices.
Serves 8

Spiced peaches
Potjie No. 2

1 onion, sliced
15 ml butter
15 ml cooking oil
5 ml ground coriander
5 ml garam masala
2 whole cloves
1 bay leaf
4 cardamom pods, crushed
2 ml salt
1 x 800 g can sliced peaches
45 ml vinegar
10 ml cornflour

Sauté onion in heated butter and oil. Add spices and salt and fry for 2 minutes. Add peaches with juice and simmer for 5 minutes. Mix vinegar and cornflour to form a paste and add to peaches. Simmer for a further 5 minutes and serve with Soutribbetjie with vegetables (page 36) or braaied meat.
Serves 6

Clockwise from left: Curried vegetables, Ratatouille in a potjie (page 79), Buttered vegetable potjie, Braaied mushrooms with garlic butter

A Vegetarian Feast

Curried vegetables

Potjie Nos. 1 and 3

30 ml cooking oil
2 large onions, sliced
4 large cloves garlic, crushed
15 ml chopped root ginger
15–30 ml medium curry powder
5 ml turmeric
2 bay leaves
5 ml salt
50 ml sultanas
2 large tomatoes, skinned and
   coarsely chopped
3 potatoes, peeled and sliced
250 g green beans,
   cut into pieces
½ cabbage, shredded
a few outside cabbage leaves
   to cover

Heat oil in small potjie. Add onion and garlic and sauté until transparent. Add ginger, curry powder, turmeric and bay leaves and fry lightly. Add salt, sultanas and tomatoes. Simmer while stirring continuously until the mixture is thick. Remove from heat and set aside.

Grease large potjie with butter. First place potatoes on the bottom. Spoon a little sauce over the potatoes and then place green beans on top of potatoes. Spoon some more sauce over. Now arrange shredded cabbage on top of beans. Spoon remaining sauce over. Arrange outside cabbage leaves over the top of the vegetables to keep them moist during the cooking process. Cover with lid and place over a slow fire for 30–45 minutes or until the vegetables are cooked.

Serves 8–10

Whole-wheat potbread

Flat-bottomed Potjie No. 3 or 4

375 ml lukewarm water
50 ml golden syrup
20 ml dried yeast
750 ml white bread flour
7 ml salt
625 ml whole-wheat flour
75 ml sunflower seed oil

Mix water and syrup together. Sprinkle yeast on top of water and allow to stand for about 10 minutes or until the mixture becomes foamy. Meanwhile sift bread flour and salt and add whole-wheat flour. Trickle oil onto dry ingredients and mix well. Add another 100 ml lukewarm water to yeast mixture. Add yeast mixture to dry ingredients and mix to a soft, manageable dough. Place dough in a warm place until doubled in size. Knock dough back. Form into a round loaf and place in greased potjie. Brush inside of lid with oil and cover potjie, then allow dough to rise to double its size. Place potjie on a small fire with a few coals on top of the lid. Bake for about 1 hour or until bread sounds hollow when tapped on the bottom.

Note: This recipe can also be used for vetkoek, roosterkoek and stokbrood.

Bread

Roosterkoek

500 ml bread flour
2 ml bicarbonate of soda
2 ml cream of tartar
2 ml salt
60 g butter or margarine
thick milk or buttermilk to make batter

Sift dry ingredients together. Cut butter into small pieces and rub into flour mixture until it resembles fine breadcrumbs. Stir in enough thick milk or buttermilk to make an easily manageable soft dough. Break off pieces of dough and shape into flat cakes. Sprinkle with lots of flour to ensure that the roosterkoek does not stick to the grid. Cook very slowly on a greased grid over glowing coals until the roosterkoek are done. Serve with butter, golden syrup, moskonfyt or jam.
Makes about 15

Variation
Brush a No. 4 flat-bottomed cast-iron potjie with oil. Heat well. Place roosterkoek into potjie and bake over a slow fire until done. Do not let the roosterkoek touch each other as they rise while baking and will stick together.

From left to right: Roosterkoek, Stokbrood (page 85), Feather-light buttermilk vetkoek (page 85), Onion bread (page 86)

HOW TO MAKE POTBROOD

Use your favourite bread recipe. If you genuinely don't have kneading hands, you can cheat, in secret, with a stir bread or buy bread dough from a bakery. Let the bread rise in a warm place – a car standing in the sun makes an excellent place for the dough to rise. Make a shallow hole in the ground just large enough for the potjie to nestle into. Make a fire, not too big, in the hole and allow it to burn until only a few glowing coals remain. Place the dough in the greased potjie and brush the top of the dough and the inside of the lid with melted butter or cooking oil. Place the potjie on the fire and put a few small coals on top of the lid. Put a piece of corrugated iron on top and shovel a bit of sand on top of the iron. Bake the bread for approximately 1 hour.

The type of wood used for your fire naturally plays an important role in the baking of bread. Some woods burn quicker than others, and therefore you might have to add more coals during the baking process. However, it is easy to slide the iron off the top of the hole, take a peek at the coals and add more if necessary. Then simply slide the iron back over the hole to finish the baking.

If it is not possible to dig a hole, the fire can be made on top of the soil, on a cement slab or on bricks. Place the potjie onto a thin layer of almost burned-out coals or alternatively the potjie can be placed on a metal stand over the coals. Place a few coals on top of the lid and bake the bread until done.

Ester's potbrood
Flat-bottomed Potjie No. 4

15 ml dried yeast
10 ml sugar
375 ml lukewarm water
500 ml lukewarm milk
45 ml golden syrup, warmed
30 ml melted butter
7 x 250 ml cake flour
2 x 250 ml white bread flour
15 ml salt
250 ml whole-wheat flour

Mix yeast, sugar and lukewarm water together and allow to stand in a warm place for about 10 minutes until foamy. Add lukewarm milk, golden syrup and butter to the yeast mixture. Sift cake flour, bread flour and salt together. Add whole-wheat flour and stir lightly. Add milk mixture to dry mixture and stir to a soft dough. Knead dough until it becomes elastic and comes away cleanly from the sides of the bowl. Place dough directly into well-greased flat-bottomed potjie. Brush lid with butter or oil and cover potjie. Allow to stand in a warm place, not too close to the fire, for about 1 hour until doubled in size. Place potjie onto a few well burnt down coals. Push some coals around potjie and place a few on the lid. Make sure that the coals are not too hot as the cast iron holds the heat for a long time and you might burn the bread. If necessary, add more coals during the baking process. When done, serve bread with butter, golden syrup, honey or jam.

Herby potbrood
Flat-bottomed Potjie No. 4

This recipe is for a stir bread, which, although not a real potbrood recipe, is so easy to make and so delicious that even a food connoisseur will not be able to tell the difference.

1 kg cake or whole-wheat flour
   (or a mixture of both)
50 ml sugar
25 ml salt
50 ml cooking oil
125 ml chopped fresh parsley
125 ml chopped celery
30 ml chopped fresh mixed
   herbs or 10 ml dried
250 g grated Cheddar cheese
200 g chopped walnuts
   (optional)
1 packet instant yeast
875 ml lukewarm water

Mix all ingredients together, except lukewarm water, in a large mixing bowl. Add water and mix to a soft batter-like consistency. Pour into greased potjie and cover with greased lid. Place near the fire and leave to rise for approximately 1 hour until doubled in size. Sprinkle a little extra cheese over the bread and place over the coals. Place a few coals on top of the lid and bake for 1$\frac{1}{4}$ hours or until the bread gives a hollow sound when tapped. Turn out as quickly as possible otherwise the crust might fall off.

Mealie bread

Flat-bottomed Potjie No. 3

500 ml whole corn kernels,
  fresh or canned
15 ml soft butter
30 ml brown sugar
1 egg, beaten
10 ml baking powder
125 ml milk
2–5 ml salt

Mix all the ingredients together thoroughly. Spoon mixture into 1 large or 2 small buttered jam tins. Cover the tins with buttered aluminium foil, shiny-side in. Place tins into potjie and carefully pour in boiling water to halfway up the sides of the tins. Cover potjie with lid and steam gently for 45–60 minutes or until bread is cooked. Allow bread to cool slightly before turning out otherwise it might break. Slice and spread with butter or rendered mutton or lard while still warm.

Stokbrood

1.2 kg white bread flour
15 ml salt
10 ml instant yeast
10 ml cooking oil
500 ml lukewarm water

Mix flour, salt and yeast. Add oil and water until it forms a stiff dough. The dough must be stiff otherwise it will slip off the stick. Knead well, put in a warm place until doubled in size, then knock back. Take a piece of dough and roll it into a long sausage shape between your hands. Wrap it around a long clean stick and pinch the end to close. Allow to rise for 15 minutes in a warm place. Braai over slow coals until done. Remove from stick, and butter generously. Add a spoon of jam if desired.

Potato bread

Flat-bottomed Potjie No. 4

1 large potato, peeled and
  cubed
6 x 250 ml cake flour or
  white bread flour
5 ml salt
1 packet instant yeast
10 ml sugar
30 ml butter or lard

Cover potato with 375 ml water and boil until tender. Remove potato from water and set water aside. Quickly mash potato finely with a fork. If you wait for it to cool down the potato is inclined to become slimy and form lumps. Add lukewarm water to the potato water to make up 500 ml and add to the mashed potato. Stir well. Sift flour and salt and add to potato mixture together with yeast and sugar. Stir carefully to form an easily manageable dough. Knead in the butter or lard. Turn dough out onto a lightly floured surface and knead for about 5 minutes until the dough becomes elastic and comes away easily from the floured surface. Place dough in well-greased potjie. Brush dough and lid with melted butter. Cover with lid and put into a warm place (not near the fire) and allow to rise for 30–40 minutes or until dough has doubled in size. Place over low heat. Put a few small coals on top of the lid and bake for 50–60 minutes or until the bread is golden brown and sounds hollow when tapped. Serve sliced with butter, lard or rendered mutton fat into which a few kaiings have been stirred.

Wine bread

375 ml self-raising flour
5 ml salt
5 ml celery seeds
80 ml cooking oil
wine to mix dough

Mix dry ingredients. Add oil and enough wine to form a soft dough. On a floured board, roll dough into thin 'pancakes'. Bake in greased cast-iron pan over the open fire.
Serves 6

Feather-light buttermilk vetkoek

Potjie No. $^3/_4$ or 1

500 ml cake flour
20 ml baking powder
3 ml salt
15–30 ml melted butter or
  cooking oil
1 egg
approx. 250 ml buttermilk
cooking oil for deep-frying

Sift flour, baking powder and salt together. Beat butter, egg and buttermilk together and stir into flour. The dough should have a spongy texture that drips easily off the spoon. Half fill potjie with cooking oil and heat until oil bubbles. Place spoonfuls of dough into the hot oil. Deep-fry for a few minutes. Turn and fry until golden brown. Remove when cooked and drain on paper towelling. Serve with butter and/or golden syrup or honey.
Makes 18–20

Stir bread

Flat-bottomed Potjie No. 3

3 x 250 ml bread flour
10 ml salt
30 ml white sugar
1 packet instant yeast
30 ml melted butter or lard
350 ml lukewarm water
coarse salt

Sift flour and salt together in a warmed mixing bowl. Add sugar and yeast and mix lightly. Stir in butter or lard. Make a hollow in the flour mixture, add water and stir until all the ingredients are mixed, stirring thoroughly for 2 minutes. Turn dough out into greased potjie. Brush dough with melted butter and sprinkle coarse salt over. Grease inside of lid and cover the potjie. Place in a warm, draughtless place for 1 hour or until the dough has doubled in size. Place the potjie on bricks or a stand over a small fire. Put a few small coals on top of the lid. Bake for 45–60 minutes or until the bread sounds hollow when tapped.

Steamed milk bread

500 g self-raising flour
1 ml baking powder
1 ml salt
310 ml milk

Sift dry ingredients. Add milk. Mix well with spatula, then knead lightly. Place in a greased pudding bowl and allow to rise slightly. Place in a potjie and pour in enough boiling water to come halfway up sides of bowl. Steam for 1¼ hours, then turn out onto a plate and cut bread into slices while still warm.
Serves 6

Mealie meal bread

Flat-bottomed Potjie No. 3 or 4

375 ml milk
500 ml mealie meal
5 ml salt
50 ml butter
3 eggs
10 ml baking powder

Heat 250 ml of the milk. Mix the remaining milk with the mealie meal. Add mealie meal and milk mixture, salt and butter to the hot milk and simmer for a few minutes. Allow to cool slightly. Beat eggs well. Stir the mealie meal mixture gradually into the eggs. Stir in baking powder. Spoon the mixture into a well-greased potjie and cover with lid. Bake over a slow fire for 30–40 minutes or until the bread is done. Serve with butter or cream cheese.

Variations
Herb bread: *Add 30 ml chopped fresh herbs or 10 ml dried mixed herbs to the mixture.*
Carrot bread: *Add 250 ml grated carrot to the mixture.*
Garlic bread: *Add 4 cloves garlic, chopped to the mixture.*
Cheese bread: *Add 250 ml grated Cheddar cheese to the mixture.*

Onion bread

Potjie No. 1 and Flat-bottomed
Potjie No. 4

6 x 250 ml white bread flour
5 ml salt
1 packet instant yeast
1 packet onion soup
30 ml sugar
2 medium onions, thinly sliced
30 ml butter or lard
550 ml lukewarm water
1 egg white, lightly beaten
cornflour
125 ml grated Cheddar cheese

Sift flour and salt together. Add yeast, soup powder and sugar. Sauté onion in heated butter or lard in smaller potjie. Remove onion and allow to cool. When cool, add to flour mixture and stir lightly. Make a hollow in the flour mixture and add the water. Mix until it forms a soft dough. Turn dough out onto a floured surface and knead for 5 minutes or until the dough is smooth. Divide dough into two pieces. Grease flat-bottomed potjie with butter and place two pieces of dough into pot. Brush dough with egg white and sprinkle a thick layer of cornflour over the top of one half of the dough and sprinkle the other half with cheese. Brush inside of lid with butter and cover potjie. Place potjie in a warm, draughtless place and allow dough to rise until doubled in size. Place the potjie on a small fire for 45–60 minutes or until bread sounds hollow when tapped.

From left to right: Onion bread, Herby potbrood (page 84)

Desserts

Potjie fondue
Potjie No. 1

1 x 100 g chocolate with nuts and raisins
1 x 100 g dark chocolate
5 ml grated orange or lemon rind
75 ml orange, apricot or peach juice
30 g butter
15 ml brandy, rum or whisky (optional)

Grease potjie with butter. Melt chocolate very slowly over a tiny fire. Remove potjie from heat for a while if it looks as thought the chocolate will burn. Add grated rind and fruit juice gradually. Continue stirring until all the ingredients are well mixed and the mixture is creamy. Do not allow the mixture to boil. Break butter into small pieces and add a few at a time while stirring. Add brandy, rum or whisky and stir until well mixed.

To serve: If a large number of guests are being entertained, make this fondue and the variation using two separate potjies. Arrange any of the following ingredients attractively on a tray.
Fruit: Peel yellow peaches, hairless mangoes, apples, pears, etc., and slice into wedges. Sprinkle with lemon juice to stop discolouration. Cherries, strawberries and litchis can be left whole.
Cake: Cubes of fruit cake, boudoir biscuits or any other firm cake.
Marshmallows: Use forks or wooden skewers to dip the goodies into the hot chocolate
Serves 6

Variation
White chocolate fondue: *Melt 200 g white chocolate in a small potjie over a tiny fire. Remove potjie from heat if there are any signs of burning. Stir in 100 ml Cape Velvet liqueur (or any other creamy liqueur) and 75 ml strawberry fruit juice or any other fresh fruit juice.*

Potjie fondue

Fruit potjie pudding

Potjie No. 3

1 kg mixed dried fruit
50 ml honey
25 ml brown sugar
1 litre apricot or orange juice
25 ml lemon juice
25 ml custard powder
25 ml cold water

MUESLI DUMPLINGS
250 ml self-raising flour
2 ml baking powder
125 ml muesli
50 ml coconut
50 ml chopped nuts
30 ml brown sugar
1 egg
approx. 250 ml natural
   yoghurt
30 ml melted butter
2 ml salt
cinnamon sugar

Mix dried fruit, honey, brown sugar, apricot or orange juice and lemon juice in a potjie. Cover with a lid and simmer for 45 minutes or until fruit is very soft. Mix custard powder and water and add to fruit.

To make the dumplings, mix dry ingredients together. Beat egg, yoghurt, melted butter and salt together and add to dry ingredients. Drop spoonfuls of dough on top of fruit. Cover with lid and simmer for about 20 minutes. Do not peep, otherwise the dumplings will collapse. Sprinkle with cinnamon sugar and serve immediately.
Serves 8–10

Variation
Omit the dumplings, if preferred.

Potjie puréed pumpkin

Flat-bottomed Potjie No. 3

500 g finely mashed cooked
   pumpkin
375 ml cake flour
2 ml salt
75 ml hot milk
15 ml melted butter
30 ml sugar
15 ml lemon juice
5 ml grated lemon rind
3 eggs, separated
pinch of salt
cinnamon sugar (optional)

Drain pumpkin well in a sieve. Sift flour and salt together. Add flour and milk alternately to mashed pumpkin and stir lightly. Add butter, sugar, lemon juice and rind to pumpkin. Add egg yolks one at a time stirring well after each addition. Add a pinch of salt to egg whites and beat until stiff. Fold beaten egg whites gently into mixture. Grease potjie well with butter or oil and spoon mixture into it. Cover with lid and place potjie over slow fire. Put a few small coals on lid to brown top of pudding. Bake for 30 minutes or until cooked. Sprinkle with cinnamon sugar and serve immediately.
Serves 6

Hint
This dish can also be served as a side dish with meat. Omit the sugar and add lemon juice, otherwise it will be too sweet.

Potjie cake

Potjie No. 1 and Flat-bottomed
Potjie No. 6

SYRUP
400 ml sugar
500 ml water
5 ml ground cinnamon
5 ml ground ginger
10 ml vanilla essence

BATTER
230 g butter
230 g smooth apricot jam
230 g dates, chopped
230 g walnuts or almonds,
   chopped
10 ml bicarbonate of soda
   mixed with 125 ml milk
1 egg, beaten
5 x 250 ml cake flour
5 ml salt

To prepare the syrup, mix sugar and water in flat-bottomed potjie and stir over low heat until sugar has dissolved. Bring to the boil, then add remaining ingredients.

To prepare the batter, melt butter and apricot jam together in the small potjie. Remove from heat and pour into mixing bowl. Stir in dates and nuts. Add bicarbonate of soda and milk mixture and egg. Sift flour and salt together and fold lightly into butter and fruit mixture to form a soft batter. Drop spoonfuls of the batter into the boiling syrup. Cover with lid and simmer very slowly for 20–30 minutes.
Serves 6

Fruit potjie pudding

Fruit under the blanket

Flat-bottomed Potjie No. 4 or 6

1 kg fresh fruit (such as cling
   peaches, plums, apricots,
   guavas, quinces or pears)
150–200 ml sugar
700 ml water
1 stick cinnamon
1 bay leaf
1 small piece lemon peel
4 black peppercorns

BATTER
125 g butter or margarine
150 ml sugar
3 eggs, beaten
300 ml cake flour
2 ml salt
10 ml baking powder
50 ml cinnamon sugar

Prepare fruit according to type. Peel peaches, quinces and pears and cut into wedges. Halve plums, apricots and guavas without peeling.

Place sugar, water and seasonings into a potjie and heat very slowly, stirring until the sugar has melted. Bring to the boil. Skim foam off top. Place fruit into boiling syrup and simmer slowly, uncovered, for 10 minutes or until fruit is barely tender. Remove seasonings.

Meanwhile, prepare the batter by creaming butter and sugar. Add eggs gradually, beating well after each addition. Sift flour, salt and baking powder together. Fold flour lightly into creamed butter and sugar. Spoon batter on top of boiling fruit mixture and cover with lid. Put a few small coals on top of lid to lightly brown batter. Bake for 30–40 minutes or until the pudding is cooked. Sprinkle with cinnamon sugar and serve hot.

Serves 8

Boer pudding

Potjie No. 1 and Flat-bottomed
Potjie No. 3

BATTER
250 g butter
250 ml sugar
3 eggs
750 ml cake flour
2 ml salt
500 ml currants
   or seedless raisins
30 g chopped almonds
50 ml chopped watermelon
   konfyt or green fig preserve
5 ml bicarbonate of soda
100 ml sour milk

BRANDY SYRUP
400 ml sugar
500 ml water
125 ml brandy
pinch of salt
2 ml ground cinnamon
1 ml grated nutmeg

To prepare batter: Cream the butter. Add sugar gradually and mix until creamy. Add eggs one at a time and beat well after each addition. Sift flour and salt together and fold gently into egg mixture. Fold currants, almonds and konfyt into batter. Dissolve bicarbonate of soda in milk and fold gently into batter. Spoon batter into a greased flat-bottomed potjie. Grease inside of lid with butter or oil and place on potjie. Place potjie over a very slow fire with a few small coals on the lid so that the top of the pudding will also brown. Bake for 30–40 minutes or until the pudding is cooked.

To prepare the syrup, mix sugar and water in a small potjie. Stir over slow heat until sugar has dissolved. Do not allow syrup to boil before sugar has dissolved. Simmer syrup for 5 minutes. Add remaining ingredients and simmer for another 2 minutes. Be careful when making syrup over coals because it boils over easily and you can get badly burned. Pour prepared syrup over pudding and leave to soak into pudding. Serve lukewarm with cream.

Serves 6

Potjie dumplings

Potjie No. 2

This delicious recipe is based on the traditional souskluitjies (cinnamon sauce dumplings) recipe.

250 ml cake flour
pinch of salt
5 ml baking powder
1 large egg, beaten
50–75 ml milk, or milk
   and water
100 ml melted butter
cinnamon sugar

Sift flour, salt and baking powder together. Beat egg, milk or milk and water and half the melted butter together and add to flour. Mix well to a soft dough that will drop easily off the spoon. Half fill potjie with water and bring to the boil. As soon as large bubbles appear in the water, drop teaspoonfuls of batter into the water. Cover with lid and simmer over a medium heat for 10 minutes. If the water boils too vigorously the mixture will boil over. Resist the temptation to peep into the potjie during this time as the dumplings will flop. After 10 minutes, if the dumplings have not yet floated to the top of the water, they are still not cooked. Replace lid and simmer for another 5 minutes. Remove dumplings from the water with a slotted spoon and place into a warm serving dish. Sprinkle with cinnamon sugar and the remaining butter. Serve and eat immediately.

Serves 10

Waterbul
Flat-bottomed Potjie No. 4

A traditional recipe that in former times was prepared on distant farms. Hence the simple ingredients.

BATTER
500 ml cake flour
5 ml baking powder
2 ml salt
140 g soft butter
5 ml ground ginger
5 ml ground cinnamon
15 ml smooth apricot jam
10 ml bicarbonate of soda
250 ml milk

SYRUP
1 litre water
300 ml sugar

To prepare the batter, sift flour, baking powder and salt together. Cream butter, add ginger, cinnamon and jam and mix well. Dissolve bicarbonate of soda in milk. Fold flour and milk alternately into butter and mix to a fairly stiff dough.

To prepare the syrup, place water and sugar into flat-bottomed potjie over a slow fire and stir until the sugar has dissolved. Bring to the boil and boil for 5 minutes.

Spoon batter into boiling syrup. Cover with lid and simmer very slowly for 1 hour or until the pudding is done. Serve with custard.
Serves 6

Vinegar pudding
Potjie No. 3

SAUCE
600 ml sugar
750 ml water
200 ml vinegar
1 stick cinnamon
1 whole clove

BATTER
60 g butter
125 ml sugar
2 eggs
375 ml cake flour
10 ml ground ginger
2 ml grated nutmeg
2 ml ground allspice
5 ml bicarbonate of soda
1 ml salt
30 ml smooth apricot jam
a little cold water for mixing
   if necessary

To prepare the sauce, mix sugar and water in potjie and stir over a small fire until sugar has dissolved. Do not allow syrup to boil before sugar has dissolved. Add vinegar and spices and boil for 5 minutes. Beware of a fire that is too hot as the syrup can easily boil over.

To prepare the batter, cream butter, add sugar gradually and mix until creamy. Do not work too close to the fire or the butter will melt. Add eggs one at a time, beating well after each addition. Sift dry ingredients together and fold lightly into creamed mixture. Stir in jam. Batter should drop off spoon easily. Add a little water if necessary. Drop spoonfuls of batter into boiling syrup. Cover with lid and put a few small coals on top of lid. Simmer very slowly for 30–40 minutes.
Serves 6

Campfire coffee with a kick
Potjie No. 2

This recipe is based on Peter Veldsman's recipe for Cape Coffee. It's a delicious drink to round off a splendid evening around the campfire. Try, however, to use pure, ground coffee and not the instant kind.

1.5 litres strong black coffee
50 ml sugar
1 orange, lemon or naartjie
   studded with 3 whole cloves
2 bay or lemon leaves
1 stick cinnamon
50 ml Van der Hum (optional)
125 ml brandy
250 ml cream (optional)
ground cinnamon to sprinkle
   on top

Place coffee, sugar, fruit studded with cloves, bay or lemon leaves and cinnamon stick into potjie. Heat over a slow fire so that the flavours blend well. Add Van der Hum. Pour brandy into a soup ladle or enamel mug. Heat carefully over the fire and set alight. Pour the flaming brandy over the coffee. Pour coffee into mugs or cups. Hold a spoon over the coffee and pour the cream very carefully onto the spoon so that the cream floats on top of the coffee. Sprinkle a little cinnamon on top and serve immediately.
Serves 5

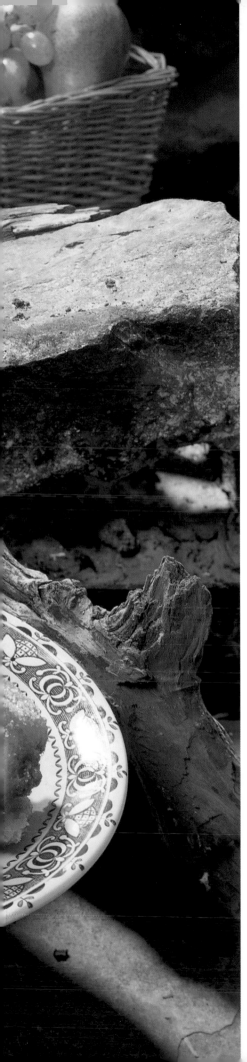

Delicious potjie pudding
Potjie No. 3

SYRUP
250 ml sugar
1 litre water

BATTER
15 ml bicarbonate of soda
250 ml smooth apricot jam
500 ml cake flour
1 ml salt
125 g butter

Prepare syrup by mixing sugar and water in the potjie over the fire. Stir until sugar dissolves before bringing it to the boil, then simmer for 5 minutes.

Prepare the batter by mixing the bicarbonate of soda and jam together. Sift flour and salt together. Cut butter into small pieces and rub into flour until it resembles fine breadcrumbs. Mix jam into flour. Spoon batter into hot syrup. Cover with lid and simmer very slowly over a small fire for 1 hour or until the pudding is done.
Serves 6

Banana vetkoek
Potjie No. 3/4 or 1

250 ml cake flour
1 ml salt
15 ml baking powder
1 egg
60 ml milk
3 bananas
15 ml lemon juice
cooking oil for deep-frying
30 ml cinnamon sugar

Sift flour, salt and baking powder together. Beat the egg into the milk. Mash the bananas and mix with lemon juice. Stir egg and milk mixture into flour. Add banana and mix well until the batter drops easily off the spoon. Half fill potjie with cooking oil and heat until the oil bubbles. Place spoonfuls of batter into the hot oil and deep-fry until golden brown and cooked. Remove from oil with a slotted spoon and drain on paper towelling. Sprinkle with cinnamon sugar and serve immediately with a wedge of lemon.
Serves 6

Dried fruit compote in a potjie
Potjie No. 2

750 g mixed dried fruit
200 ml each dry white wine
   and water
1 stick cinnamon
30 ml orange liqueur
250 ml orange juice
30 ml lemon juice
2 whole cloves
1 piece orange peel
4 crushed cardamom pods
30 ml butter

Mix all the ingredients together, except butter, and soak overnight or for a few hours in any container that will not react with the acid of the fruit. Melt butter in a potjie. Add soaked fruit, cover with lid and simmer for 20–30 minutes or until fruit is tender. Remove seasonings and serve hot or cold as dessert or add more lemon juice and serve as a side dish with meat.
Serves 6

From back to front: Dried fruit compote in a potjie, Banana vetkoek

Index

Page numbers in *italic* text refer to photographs.